Practice and Homework Journal

Grade K

Printed in the U.S.A.

ISBN 978-0-358-10576-3

5 6 7 8 9 10   0928   28 27 26 25 24 23 22 21

4500821027   C D E F G

Count Sequence and Numbers to 5

Module 4 Classify, Count, and Sort Objects

Module 5 Add To and Take From Within 5

Module 6 Put Together and Take Apart Within 5

© Houghton Mifflin Harcourt Publishing Company

Unit 2 Count Sequence and Numbers to 10

© Houghton Mifflin Harcourt Publishing Company

Unit 3 Geometry

Unit 4 Number and Operations in Base Ten

Unit 5 Measurement

Name _____

Represent 1 and 2

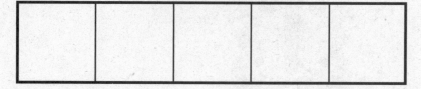

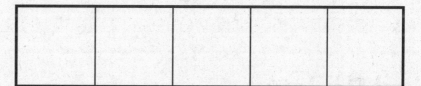

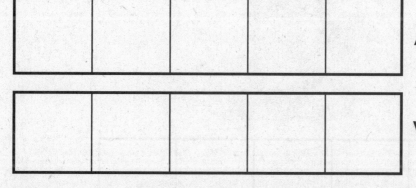

Amy

Vera

---

1. Listen to the story. How can you use a counter to represent each rabbit? *There are two rabbits in the grass.*

2. Listen to the story. How can you use a counter to represent each bird? Trace the number you represented. *One bird is flying.*

3. Listen to the story. Draw a counter to represent each crayon. *Amy has one crayon. Vera has two crayons.*

Test Prep

1   2   3
○   ○   ○

Spiral Review

 Count the puppies in each group. Circle the group that shows two puppies.

 Mark below the number that shows how many butterflies.

 Listen to the story. Draw a counter to represent each squirrel. Say each number as you represent it. *There is one squirrel looking for acorns.*

Name _____

Represent 3 and 4

3   4

1. Listen to the story. Use a counter to represent each object in the story. Say each number as you draw the counters in the five frame. Circle the number you represented. *Ty has three kites.*

2. What can you tell about the number of objects in each group? Trace the numbers.

Test Prep

2   3   4

○   ○   ○

2   3   4

Spiral Review

3 Mark below the number that shows how many frogs.
4 Circle the number that shows how many fish.
5 Listen to the story. Use a counter to represent each bird. Say each number as you draw the counters in the five frame. *There are two birds on the sidewalk.*

Name _____

Represent 5

 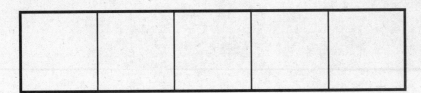

4

5

 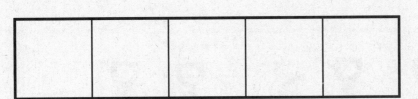

3

4

 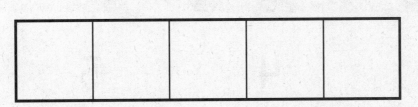

5

4

 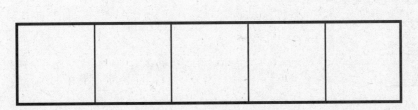

3

4

© Houghton Mifflin Harcourt Publishing Company

Listen to the story. Use a counter to represent each object in the story. Say each number as you draw the counters in the five frame. Circle the number you represented.

1 *Liane sees five starfish.*

2 *Raul sees four crabs.*

3 *Myra sees five shells.*

4 *Jac sees three seagulls.*

Circle the five frames that show five counters.

Test Prep

2   3   4

◯   ◯   ◯

3   4   5

Spiral Review

© Houghton Mifflin Harcourt Publishing Company

5️⃣ Mark below the number that shows how many sand castles.
6️⃣ Circle the number that shows how many shovels.
7️⃣ Trace the number. Use objects to represent the number. Draw the objects. Count and tell how many.

Name _____

LESSON 1.4
**More Practice/
Homework**

ONLINE
Video Tutorials and
Interactive Examples

Represent 0

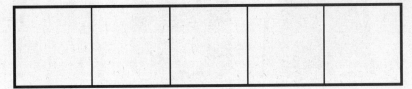

© Houghton Mifflin Harcourt Publishing Company

1. Listen to the story. Trace the number. Use a counter to represent each object in the story. Draw the counters in the five frame. *Tam has five pencils.*

Listen to the story. Use objects to represent the toy trucks. Say the number you represented. Trace the number.

2. *Pierre has four toy trucks.*

3. *Maya has three toy trucks. She gives the trucks to her brother. How many toy trucks does Maya have now?*

4. Listen to the story. Circle to show which bag holds Yolanda's marbles. *Ryan has some marbles and Yolanda has zero marbles.*

Test Prep

2　　　　　　　4　　　　　　　5
○　　　　　　　○　　　　　　　○

0　　　　　　　2　　　　　　　4
○　　　　　　　○　　　　　　　○

Spiral Review

 Mark below the number that shows how many backpacks.

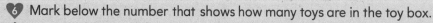 Mark below the number that shows how many toys are in the toy box.

Trace the number. Use objects to represent the number. Draw the objects. Count and tell how many.

LESSON 1.5
**More Practice/
Homework**

🍎Ed **ONLINE**
Video Tutorials and
Interactive Examples

Name _____

Ways to Make 5

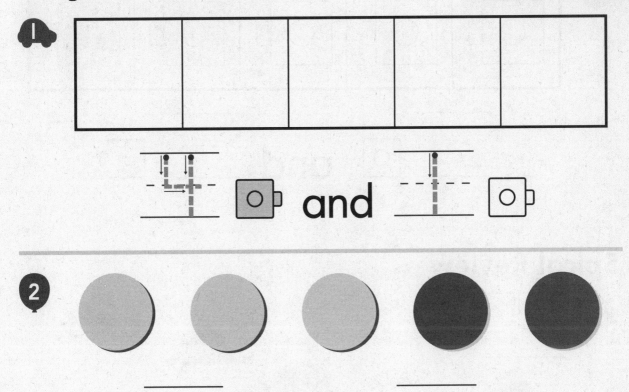

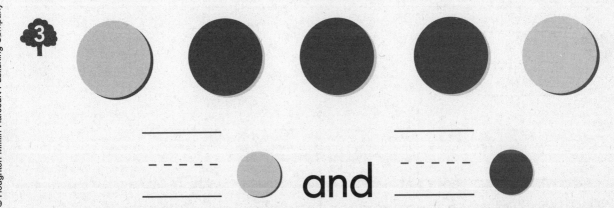

© Houghton Mifflin Harcourt Publishing Company

1. Draw in the five frame to represent the number of gray cubes and the number of white cubes. Trace the numbers. Say the numbers that make 5.

2 – 3 Write the numbers to represent the counters. Say the numbers that make 5.

Module 1 • Lesson 5

nine **P9**

Test Prep

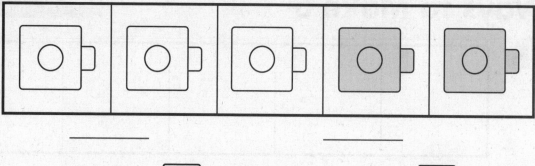

_____   and   _____

Spiral Review

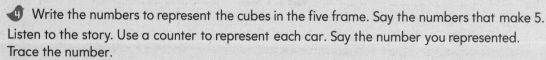

🐦 Write the numbers to represent the cubes in the five frame. Say the numbers that make 5. Listen to the story. Use a counter to represent each car. Say the number you represented. Trace the number.

⭐ Amir has some toy cars. How many toy cars does Amir have?

💙 Mei has some toy cars. She gives them to her brother. How many toy cars does Mei have now?

LESSON 2.1
**More Practice/
Homework**

ONLINE
Video Tutorials and
Interactive Examples

Name _____

Count and Write 0 and 1

 1

_____
- - - - -
_____   _____
                                    - - - - -

 2

   _____
                                    - - - - -

 3

1 Count how many caterpillars on each leaf. Write each number.
2 How many turtles are on the log? Write the number.
3 Say the number. Circle the branch that shows that number of birds.

Test Prep

0	1	2
○	○	○

_ _ _ _ _ _ _

Spiral Review

4. Mark below the number that shows how many marbles.
5. How many marbles are in the bag? Write the number.
6. Listen to the story. Draw a counter to represent each crayon. Say the number you represented. Trace the number. *Ty has three crayons.*

Name _____

Count and Write 2 and 3

 3

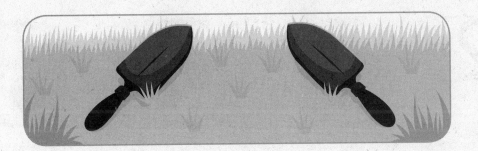

_ _ _ _ _ _

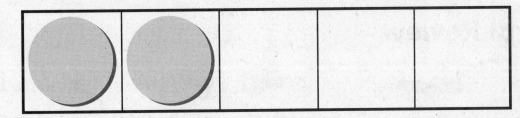

_ _ _ _ _ _

1. Say the number. Circle the bush that shows that number of butterflies.
2. Count how many tools. Write the number.
3. How many counters are in the five frame? Write the number. Draw to show what you know about the number.

Test Prep

4

_____

- - - - - - - - - -

_____

5

2

○   ○   ○

Spiral Review

 6

© Houghton Mifflin Harcourt Publishing Company

---

4 Count how many birdhouses. Write the number.

5 Say the number. Mark below the bag that has that many marbles.

6 Count how many in each group. Circle the group that shows five.

Name _____

Count and Write 4 and 5

 1

_____
- - - - - -
_____

 **2**

_____
- - - - - -
_____

 3

 4

 4

_____
- - - - - -

---

1 – **2** How many marbles are there? Write the number.
3 Say the number. Circle the group of cars that represents the number.
4 Count how many buckets. Point to each bucket as you count. Write the number.

Test Prep

5

_____

- - - - -

_____

♥ 6

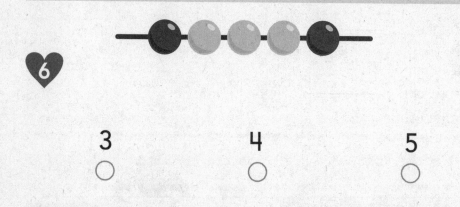

3   4   5

○   ○   ○

Spiral Review

7

---

5   Count how many baseball players. Point to each player as you count. Write the number.

♥   Count the beads. Mark below the number that shows how many.

7   Circle the two groups of toys that show ways to make five. For each group, say the two numbers that make five.

Name _____

Count and Write Numbers to 5

 1

_____
- - - - - - -
_____

 2

_____
- - - - - - -
_____

 3

_____
- - - - - - -
_____

 4

0

 5

5

 6

2

1–**3** Point to each cap as you count. Write the number that represents how many caps.
4–**6** Say the number. Circle a group of objects to represent the number.

Test Prep

_____   _____   _____

- - - - -   - - - - -   - - - - -

_____   _____   _____

_____   _____   _____

- - - - -   - - - - -   - - - - -

_____   _____   _____

Spiral Review

_____

- - - - -

_____

- - - - -

---

7. Count the markers in each group. Write the numbers to represent each group of markers.

8. Count the flowers in each picture. Write the numbers to represent each group of flowers.

Use counters to represent the story. Say the number you represented. Write the number.

9. *Miguel has some marbles in a bag.*

10. *Miguel gives his marbles to a friend. How many marbles are in the bag now?*

Name _____

Count and Order to 5

Point as you count the first cube. Trace the number. Point as you count the cubes in each group. Write the unknown numbers. Point as you count the last group of cubes. Trace the number. Say the numbers in counting order.

Test Prep

 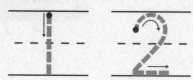

 3, 2, 5, 1, 4   1, 2, 3, 4, 5   4, 5, 1, 3, 2

○   ○   ○

Spiral Review

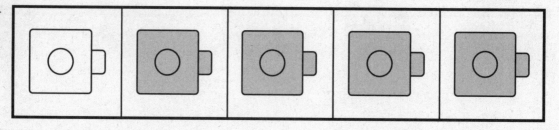

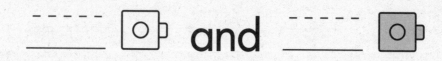

_____ _____ and _____ _____

2   Trace the numbers in order from 1 to 5.

3   Mark under the group of numbers that shows 1 to 5 in counting order.

4   Write the numbers to represent the cubes in the five frame. Say the numbers that make 5.

Name _____

Identify a Greater Number of Objects Within 5

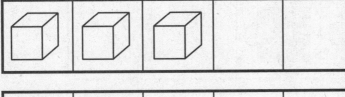

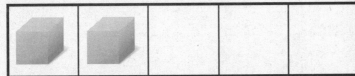

 Jane

4
- - - - -

_____

Robby

_____

---

1. Listen to the story. How can you represent the groups of objects? Circle the group that has the greater number of cubes. *Paul has five gray cubes. He also has four white cubes.*

2. Listen to the story. Place objects to match the story. Identify the group that has the greater number of blocks. Circle that group. *Rachelle has three white blocks. She also has two gray blocks.*

3. *Jane has a number of model cars that is one greater than Robby. Jane has four cars. How many cars does Robby have? Draw to show Robby's cars. Write the number of cars that Robby has.*

Test Prep

 4

5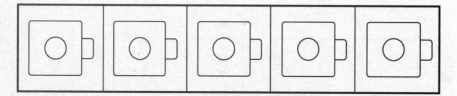

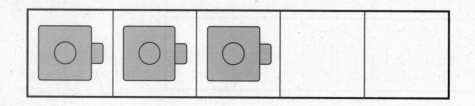

Spiral Review

6

3   4

© Houghton Mifflin Harcourt Publishing Company

4 Listen to the story. Identify the group that has the greater number of cubes.
   Circle that group. *Suri has one gray cube. She also has three white cubes.*

5 Look at the group of white cubes and the group of gray cubes. Circle the group
   with the greater number of objects.

6 How many flowers are there? Circle the number.

Name _____

Identify a Lesser Number of Objects Within 5

---

 2 Don

....

Eddie

_____
- - - - -
_____

....

Fred

_____
- - - - -
_____

🔊 Listen to the story. How can you represent the groups of objects? Circle the group with the number of objects that is less than the other group. *Alicia has four white cubes. She also has two gray cubes.*

2 *Don, Eddie, and Fred each have a number. Don's number is 5. Eddie's number is one less than Don's number. Fred's number is one less than Eddie's number. What numbers do Eddie and Fred have? Use counters or draw to find the answer. Write the numbers.*

Test Prep

Spiral Review

---

3 Listen to the story. Place cubes to match the story. Identify the group with the number of objects that is less than the other group. Circle that group. *Jonas has four gray cubes. He also has one white cube.*

4 Compare the groups of cubes. Circle the group with the lesser number of objects.

5 Count how many jump ropes. Write the number.

Name

Match Equal Groups of Objects Within 5

```
┌─────┬─────┬─────┬─────┬─────┐
│     │     │     │     │     │
└─────┴─────┴─────┴─────┴─────┘

┌─────┬─────┬─────┬─────┬─────┐
│     │     │     │     │     │
└─────┴─────┴─────┴─────┴─────┘
```

```
┌─────┬─────┬─────┬─────┬─────┐
│     │     │     │     │     │
└─────┴─────┴─────┴─────┴─────┘

┌─────┬─────┬─────┬─────┬─────┐
│     │     │     │     │     │
└─────┴─────┴─────┴─────┴─────┘
```

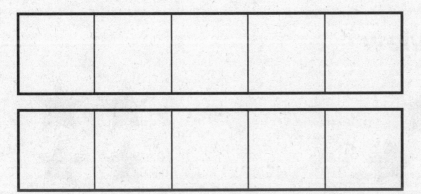

1. Draw counters to represent the apples and oranges in the five frames. Match the number of apples to the number of oranges and describe the groups using *greater than*, *less than*, or *equal to*.
2. Listen to the story. Draw a counter to represent each toy car. Compare and match the groups. *Samuel has four toy cars. Kevin has four toy cars. Who has the greater number of toy cars?*

Test Prep

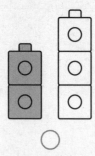   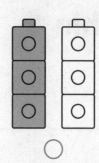   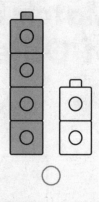

Spiral Review

© Houghton Mifflin Harcourt Publishing Company

3   Mark under the picture that shows a number of white cubes that is equal to the number of gray cubes.

4   Count the number of counters. Draw and match to show an equal number of objects.

5   Identify the group that has the greater number of stars. Circle that group.

Name _____

Compare Groups Within 5 by Counting

 1

_ _ _ _ _ _ 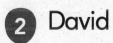   _____ _ _ _ _ _ _____

---

2 David

Joan

Lynn   _____
                                             _ _ _ _ _
                                             _____

🚗 Count the number of animals in each group. Write the numbers. Circle the number that is greater than the other number.

🎈 David has four crayons. Joan has three crayons. The number of crayons Lynn has is two less than the number David has. How many crayons does Lynn have? Draw Lynn's crayons. Write the number.

Test Prep

_____

- - - - - - - -

_____

_____

- - - - - - - -

_____

 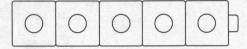

_____

- - - - - - - -

_____

Spiral Review

_____

- - - - - - - -

_____

© Houghton Mifflin Harcourt Publishing Company

3. Count the cubes in each group. Write the numbers of cubes. Circle the number that is less than the other number.

4. Draw a number of objects that is equal to the number of cubes. Write the numbers.

5. Count the birds on the branch. Write the number.

Name _____

Compare Groups Within 5 by Matching

 1

- - - - - -
_____

- - - - - -
_____

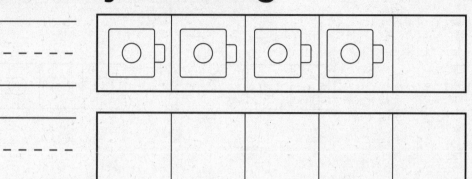

2

- - - - -
_____

1 Listen to the story. How can you represent the story using cubes to compare and match? *Jin has four baskets of apples. Rita has a number of baskets one greater than Jin.* Draw to show Rita's baskets. Write the numbers.

2 Draw a number of objects that is less than the number of cubes shown. Write the number.

Test Prep

 3

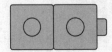

○   ○   ○

 4

   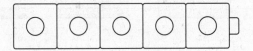

Spiral Review

 5

---

3 Count the gray cubes. Mark below the picture that shows a number of white cubes that is greater than the number of gray cubes.

4 Count the gray cubes. Circle the picture that shows a number of white cubes that is less than the number of gray cubes.

5 Count the apples. Draw and match to show an equal number of oranges.

Name _____

Compare Numbers Within 5

 1 2   3

2 4   3

3 2   5

4 4   5

1 – 2 Look at the numbers. Think about the counting order. Which number is greater? Circle the greater number.

3 – 4 Look at the numbers. Think about the counting order. Which number is less? Circle the number that is less.

Test Prep

 3 | 1 ○   4 ○   5 ○

 4 | 5 ○   3 ○   2 ○

Spiral Review

7

_____
- - - - -
_____

5 Mark below the number that is less than 3.

6 Mark below the number that is greater than 4.

7 Count how many beach balls. Write the number.

Name _____

LESSON 4.1
**More Practice/
Homework**

 ONLINE
Video Tutorials and
Interactive Examples

Classify and Count
by Color

White	Gray	Black

_____ cubes   _____ cubes   _____ cubes

⚠ Listen to the story. Look at the color categories. Classify the cubes by color
and draw the cubes in each category. Write the total number of cubes in
each category. *Jenna has five cubes. She classifies the cubes by color.
How many cubes does Jenna have of each color?*

Test Prep

2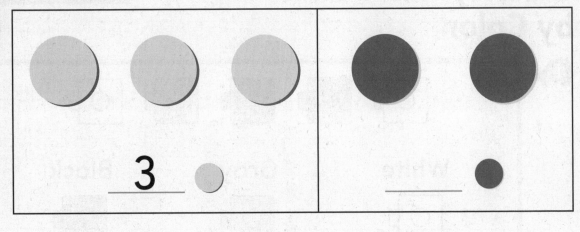

           2   4   5
            ○   ○   ○

3

           2   3   5
            ○   ○   ○

Spiral Review

4

                                               _____

                                               - - - - -

                                             _____

2 Classify the counters by color. Mark below the number that shows how many black counters there are.

3 Mark below the number that shows how many gray stars there are.

4 How many counters are there? Write the number.

Name _____

LESSON 4.2
**More Practice/
Homework**

ⓔd ONLINE
Video Tutorials and
Interactive Examples

Classify and Count
by Shape

🔎 Look at the shapes at the top of the page. Classify the shapes. Draw to show the
shapes in each category. Write the number of shapes in each category.

Test Prep

2

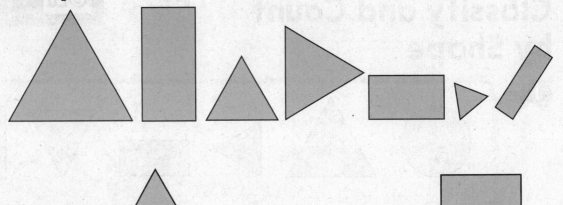

_____ 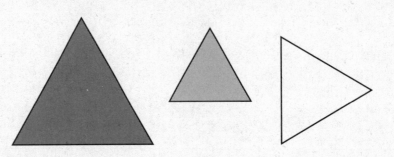   _____

3

    ○   ○   ○

Spiral Review

4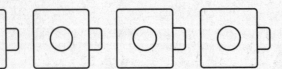

_____
- - - - - - -
_____

---

2 Write the number of shapes in each category.

3 Mark below the shape that belongs in this category.

4 Count the cubes. Write the number that represents how many cubes.

LESSON 4.3
**More Practice/
Homework**

🍊Ed **ONLINE**
Video Tutorials and
Interactive Examples

Classify and Count by Size

1 🚗

Big

_____ shapes

Small

_____ shapes

2 🎈

Big

_____

Small

_____

🚗 Listen to the story. How can you classify Luke's shapes? How many shapes are in each group? Write the number of shapes in each category. *Luke has several shapes. Some shapes are big and the rest are small.*

2 Listen to the story. Classify the objects by size. Write the number of objects in each category. *Anya has some classroom objects. She wants to know how many objects are big and how many are small.*

Test Prep

 3

Big   **Small**

_____ buttons   __2__ buttons

     2   4   5

     ○   ○   ○

 4

        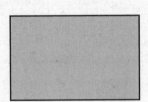

    1   3   4

    ○   ○   ○

Spiral Review

5   **4**   **5**

---

3 Mark below the number that shows how many big buttons there are.

4 Mark below the number that shows how many small shapes there are.

5 Circle the greater number.

LESSON 4.4
**More Practice/
Homework**

Ed **ONLINE**
Video Tutorials and
Interactive Examples

Classify, Count, and Sort by Count

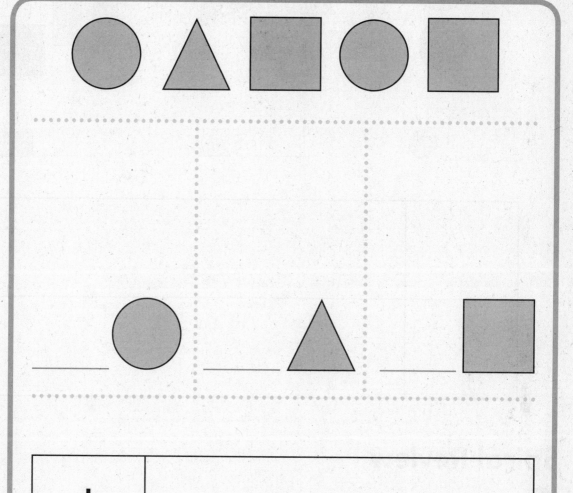

1	
2	

⚫ Classify the shapes. Write the number of shapes in each category. Sort the categories by count.

thirty-nine **P39**

Test Prep

2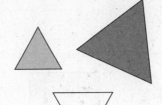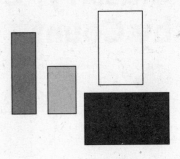

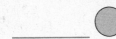  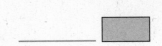

Spiral Review

© Houghton Mifflin Harcourt Publishing Company

2 Write the number of shapes in each category. Draw in the chart to show the categories sorted by count.

3 How many butterflies are there? Write the number.

LESSON 5.1
**More Practice/
Homework**

ONLINE
Video Tutorials and
Interactive Examples

Act Out Addition Problems Within 5

 1

_____ and _____ is _____

2

_____ and _____ is _____

1 How can you act out an addition problem to match the picture? Write the number in each group. Write the total.

2 Listen to the addition word problem. Act out and draw a quick picture to represent the problem. Write the number in each group. Write the total. _Two children are sitting on a rug. One more child joins them. How many children are sitting on the rug now?_

Test Prep

3	4	5
○	○	○

Spiral Review

© Houghton Mifflin Harcourt Publishing Company

3   Listen to the addition word problem. *Two children are playing. Two more children join them.* Mark under the number that represents the total number of children.

4   Circle the group that shows two turtles.

LESSON 5.2
**More Practice/
Homework**

Ed ONLINE
Video Tutorials and
Interactive Examples

Act Out Subtraction Problems Within 5

 1

_____ take away _____ is _____

2

_____ take away _____ is _____

1 Listen to the subtraction word problem. Act out and draw a quick picture to represent the problem. Write the numbers that represent the problem. *Five children are at the block center. One girl leaves. How many children are left?*

2 How can you act out a subtraction problem to match the picture? Write the numbers that represent the subtraction.

Test Prep

2   3   4
○   ○   ○

Spiral Review

_____

 Listen to the subtraction word problem. *Four children are playing in the sandbox. Two children leave.* Mark under the number that represents how many children are in the sandbox now.

 Write the number that shows how many fish.

Name _____

Solve Add To Problems Within 5

_____ **+** _____

2

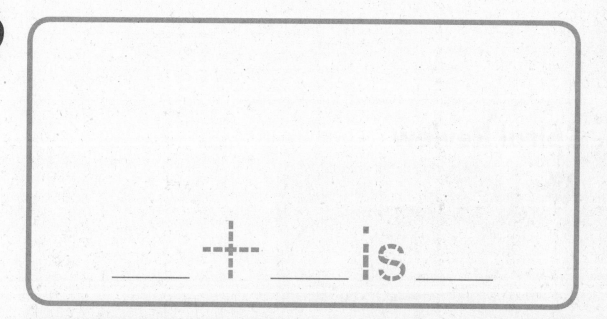

_____ **+** _____ **is** _____

---

1. Listen to the addition word problem. Use objects to represent the addition.
Write the numbers to represent how many are in each group. Trace the sign.
Four children are playing soccer. One more child comes to play.

2. Listen to the addition word problem. Use objects or drawings to represent the
problem. Complete the number sentence to model the problem. *Two birds are
on a dock. Two more birds join them. How many birds are on the dock now?*

© Houghton Mifflin Harcourt Publishing Company

Test Prep

2	3	4
○	○	○

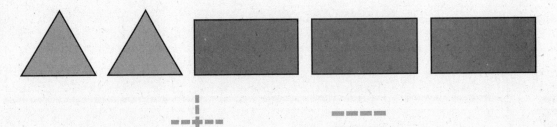

$$\underline{\hspace{2cm}} + \underline{\hspace{2cm}} = \underline{\hspace{2cm}}$$

Spiral Review

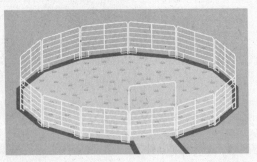

$$\underline{\hspace{2cm}}$$

 Listen to the addition word problem. *There are three apples in the bag. An orange is placed in the bag.* Mark under the number that shows how many apples and oranges are in the bag now.

 Listen to the problem. Complete the equation to model the problem. *Kina has two shapes. Then she gets three more shapes. How many shapes does Kina have now?*

 Write the number to show how many horses are in the pen.

© Houghton Mifflin Harcourt Publishing Company

Name _____

Solve Take From Problems Within 5

‗‗‗‗
_____ _____

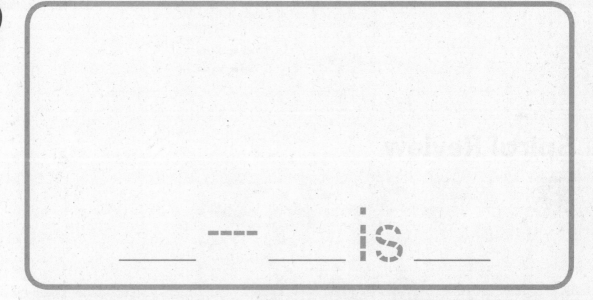

_____ ‗‗ _____ **is** _____

---

1. Listen to the subtraction word problem. Use objects to represent the subtraction. Write the numbers to represent the total and how many leave. Trace the sign. *Five children are sitting at a table in the school cafeteria. One child leaves to return to the classroom.*

2. Listen to the subtraction word problem. Use objects or drawings to represent the problem. Mark an X to show the objects being taken from the group. Complete the number sentence to model the problem. *Four squirrels are collecting acorns. Two squirrels leave. How many squirrels are still collecting acorns?*

Module 5 • Lesson 4   forty-seven **P47**

Test Prep

1	3	4
◯	◯	◯

_____   _____   _____

Spiral Review

3 Listen to the subtraction word problem. *Four cats are on the rug. Three cats leave.* Mark under the number that represents how many cats are on the rug now.

4 Listen to the subtraction word problem. Complete the equation to model the problem. *There are five kites in the sky. Two of the kites fall to the ground. How many kites are in the sky now?*

5 Circle the group that shows three ducks.

Name _____

Write Addition Equations Within 5

_____ ◯ _____ ◯ _____

2

_____ ◯ _____ ◯ _____

Listen to the addition word problem. Write an equation to model the problem.

1 *Two elephants are drinking water. Then one more elephant comes to drink water. How many elephants are drinking water now?*

2 *I saw two boats sailing on one side of the lake. Then I saw some more boats on the other side of the lake. I saw five boats on the lake. How many boats did I see on the other side of the lake?*

Test Prep

3

2	3	4
○	○	○

4

_____ ◯ _____ ◯ _____

Spiral Review

5

---

3 Listen to the addition word problem. *One bird is on the branch. Two more birds fly to the branch.* Mark under the number that shows how many birds there are now.

4 Listen to the addition word problem. Write an equation to model the problem. *One tiger is sitting. Three more tigers join it. How many tigers are there now?*

5 Compare the number of bear stickers with the number of flower stickers. Circle the group with the number of objects less than the other group.

Write Subtraction Equations Within 5

_____ ◯ _____ _____

2

_____ ◯ _____ ◯ _____

Listen to the subtraction word problem. Mark an X to show the objects being taken from the group. Write an equation to model the problem.

1 *Four cows are in the field. Three cows leave to go back to the barn. How many cows are in the field now?*

2 *I saw five seashells on the sand. Bobby took some from the group. Now there is one seashell left. How many shells did Bobby take?*

Test Prep

2   3   4
○   ○   ○

Spiral Review

_____ small beans   _____ big beans

3️⃣ Listen to the subtraction word problem. *Four chickens are in the barnyard. Two chickens leave.* Mark under the number that shows how many chickens there are now.

4️⃣ Write the number that shows how many beans are in each group.

Name _____

LESSON 5.7
**More Practice/
Homework**

ONLINE
Video Tutorials and
Interactive Examples

Solve Result Unknown Word Problems Within 5

_____ ◯ _____ ◯ _____

_____ ◯ _____ ◯ _____

Listen to the word problem. Show how to solve the problem. Write the equation to model the problem.

1 *There are three children at the playground. One more child joins. How many children are at the playground now?*

2 *There are five bikes in the bike rack. Three children get on their bikes and ride off. How many bikes are left?*

Test Prep

3 + 1 = 4   3 + 2 = 5   4 − 3 = 1
   ◯   ◯   ◯

Spiral Review

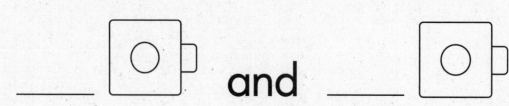

____   and   ____

3 Listen to the problem. *Three children are riding their bikes. One more child joins them.* Mark under the equation that shows how many children there are now.

4 Color some of the cubes in the cube train red and some of them blue to show a way to make five. Color one cube in the sentence red. Color the other cube in the sentence blue. Write the numbers to show how many of each color you used to represent 5.

Name _____

LESSON 6.1
More Practice/Homework

ONLINE
Video Tutorials and
Interactive Examples

Represent Addition Problems Within 5 Using Objects and Drawings

_____

_____

_____

1. Listen to the addition word problem. How can you use objects or drawings to represent the problem? Write the number that answers the question in the problem. *There are two black fish and three white fish. How many fish are there?*

Listen to the addition word problem. Draw quick pictures to represent the problem. Write the answer to the question in the problem.

2. *There are three apples and one banana in the basket. How many pieces of fruit are in the basket?*

3. *Eli has three orange cubes and two yellow cubes. How many cubes does Eli have?*

Test Prep

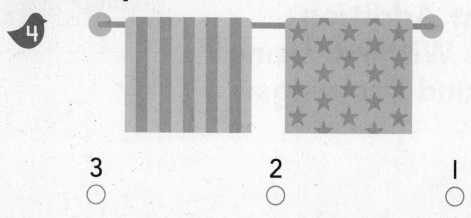

3   2   1
○   ○   ○

3   4

Spiral Review

4️⃣ Listen to the addition word problem. Mark below the number that answers the question. *There is one towel with stripes and one towel with stars on the rack. How many towels are on the rack?*

5️⃣ Listen to the addition word problem. Use the drawing that represents the problem. Circle the number that answers the question. *There are three shirts and one pair of pants on the clothesline. How many pieces of clothing are on the line?*

6️⃣ Compare the groups of lamps. Circle the group that has a number of lamps that is less than the other group.

LESSON 6.2
**More Practice/
Homework**

ONLINE
Video Tutorials and
Interactive Examples

Name _____

Represent Subtraction Problems Within 5 Using Objects and Drawings

_____

②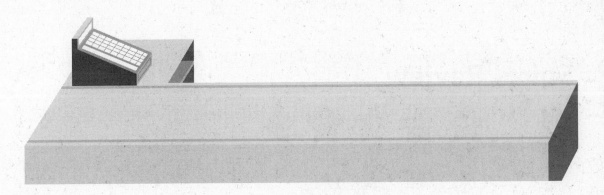

_____

Listen to the subtraction word problem. Draw quick pictures to represent the problem. Write the answer to the question in the problem.

① *Molly has five cars. Two of the cars are yellow. The rest are blue. How many cars are blue?*

② *There are five items on the counter. Three items are limes. The rest are lemons. How many are lemons?*

Test Prep

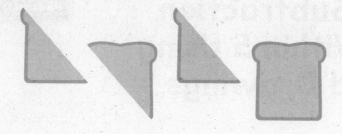

4   3   1
○   ○   ○

1   2

Spiral Review

 Listen to the subtraction word problem. Mark below the number that answers the question. *There are four pieces of bread. Three are sliced. The rest are whole. How many pieces of bread are whole?*

 Listen to the subtraction word problem. Circle the number that answers the question. *There are three fruits and vegetables. Two are carrots. The rest are pineapples. How many are pineapples?*

 Compare the groups of stars. Circle the group with a number of objects that is greater than the other group.

Name _____

Solve Put Together Problems Within 5

_____ + _____   _____ = _____

_____ + _____   _____ = _____

_____ ◯ _____ ◯ _____

Listen to the addition word problem. How can you use objects or drawings to solve the problem? Complete the equation to model the problem.

1 *There are two forks and two spoons. How many utensils are there?*

2 *The toy store has one basketball and one football. How many sports balls does the toy store have?*

Listen to the word problem as you look at the picture. Write the equation to model how many in each group are put together. Solve the problem.

3 *There is one hairbrush and three toothbrushes on the sink. How many brushes are there?*

Test Prep

$3 + 2 = 5$ ○ $2 + 2 = 4$ ○ $3 + 1 = 4$ ○

_____ _____ 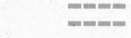 _____

Spiral Review

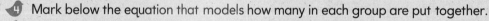

4. Mark below the equation that models how many in each group are put together.

5. Listen to the addition word problem as you look at the picture. Complete the equation to model the problem. *There are two books with a star on the cover and one book with a flower on the cover. How many books are there?*

6. Count the number of butterflies. Draw to show an equal number of objects.

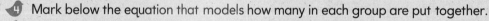

Name _____

Solve Take Apart Problems Within 5

1

----   ---- ----

_____   _____   _____

2

----   ---- ---- ----

_____   _____   _____

3

_____ ◯ _____ ◯ _____

Listen to the subtraction word problem. How can you use objects or drawings to solve the problem? Complete the equation to model the problem.

1 *There are five socks. Two socks are plain. The rest have stripes. How many socks have stripes?*

2 *There are two windows. One window is open. The rest are closed. How many windows are closed?*

Listen to the word problem as you look at the picture. Write the equation to model how the group is being taken apart. Solve the problem.

3 *There are four kittens. One kitten is playing. The rest are sleeping. How many kittens are sleeping?*

Test Prep

$$5 - 2 = 3 \qquad 5 - 4 = 1 \qquad 5 - 5 = 0$$

○   ○   ○

_____ ◯ _____ ◯ _____

Spiral Review

4

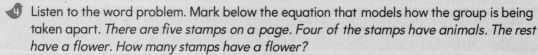

4   Listen to the word problem. Mark below the equation that models how the group is being taken apart. *There are five stamps on a page. Four of the stamps have animals. The rest have a flower. How many stamps have a flower?*

5   Listen to the word problem as you look at the picture. Write the equation to model how the group is being taken apart. Solve the problem. *There are three shoes. Two are sandals. The rest are boots. How many of the shoes are boots?*

6   Draw to represent the number.

LESSON 6.5
**More Practice/
Homework**

ONLINE
Video Tutorials and
Interactive Examples

Name

Represent Addition Using Mental Images

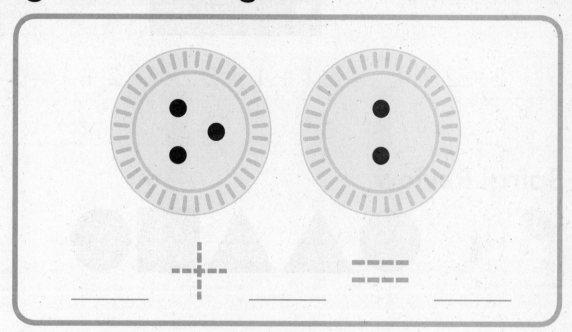

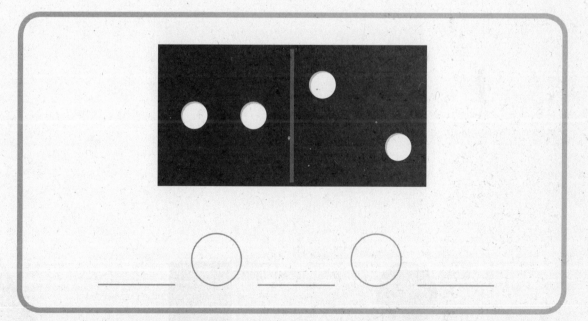

1. Look at the dot plates. Without counting, complete the equation to model the groups of dots being put together.
2. Look at the domino. Without counting, write the equation to model the groups of dots being put together.

Test Prep

2 + 2 = 4   1 + 1 = 2   2 + 1 = 3
     ○   ○   ○

Spiral Review

 Mark below the equation that models the groups of dots being put together.

 Look at the shapes at the top of the problem. Draw to show the shapes in each category. Write the total number of shapes in each category.

Name _____

Represent Subtraction Using Mental Images

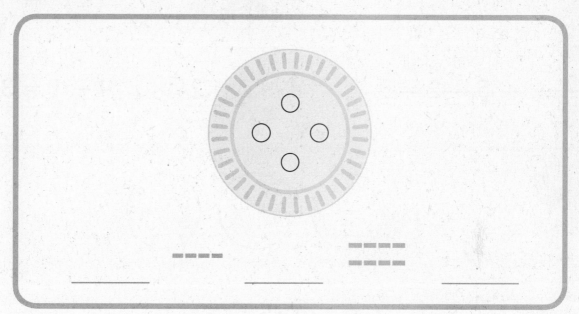

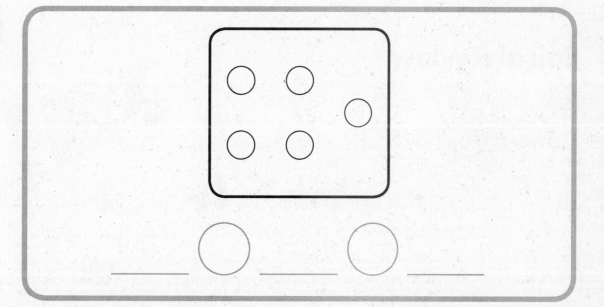

1. Look at the dot plate. How can you represent the subtraction? Complete the equation to model the subtraction problem. *What if one dot is blue and the rest are green? How many dots are green?*

2. Look at the dot card. Write the equation to model the subtraction problem. *What if three of the dots are yellow, and the rest are red? How many dots are red?*

Test Prep

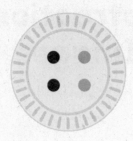

$$5 - 2 = 3 \qquad 4 - 2 = 2 \qquad 4 - 1 = 3$$
○   ○   ○

_____   _____   _____

Spiral Review

 _____   _____

---

3. Look at the dot plate. Mark below the equation that models the subtraction problem. *There are four dots. Two of the dots are gray. The rest are black. How many dots are black?*

4. Look at the counters. Write the equation to model the subtraction problem. *What if one counter is red and the rest are yellow? How many counters are yellow?*

5. Count the objects in each group. Write the numbers. Circle the number that is less than the other number.

Name _____

Solve Word Problems Within 5

1

2

Listen to the word problem. Write the equation to model the problem. Solve the problem.

1 *There are two striped fish and one spotted fish. How many fish are there?*

2 *There are four balloons. Two of the balloons are blue. The rest are green. How many balloons are green?*

Test Prep

$$2 + 3 = 5 \qquad 1 + 4 = 5 \qquad 5 - 1 = 4$$
◯ ◯ ◯

_____ ◯ _____ ◯ _____

Spiral Review

_____ _____ _____

 Listen to the word problem. Mark below the equation that models the problem. Solve the problem. *Lena has two pineapples and three bananas. How many fruits does Lena have?*

 Listen to the word problem. Write the equation to model the problem. Solve the problem. *Ali has five pens. One pen is red. The rest are blue. How many pens are blue?*

 Count the marbles in each bag. Write the number.

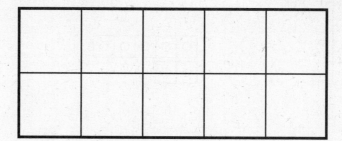
Name _____

Represent 6 and 7

 1

 2

 3

6　　　　**7**

1 *Mel has six cats.* How can you use objects to represent each cat? Draw counters to show the number of cats. Say the number. Trace the number.

2 Count the trucks in each group. Circle the groups that have seven trucks.

3 *Chan picks six apples.* Draw to show the apples. Circle the number that represents the group of apples.

Test Prep

   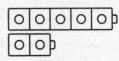   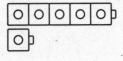

○   ○   ○

Spiral Review

_____

 Count the cubes in each group. Mark under the group that has six cubes.

 Trace the number. Draw to represent the number. Say the number.

 There is one apple in a bag. Circle the picture that shows that bag. Write the number.

LESSON 7.2
**More Practice/
Homework**

 ONLINE
Video Tutorials and
Interactive Examples

Represent 8 and 9

 1

8   9

2

---

1 *There are nine children who want to play a tambourine.* Draw a tambourine for each of them. Circle the number that represents the group of tambourines.

2 Count the bells in each group. Circle the group that has eight bells.

Test Prep

 3

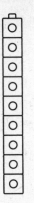  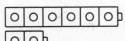

○ ○ ○

 4

Spiral Review

 5

_____ ◯ _____ ◯ _____

3 Count the cubes in each group. Mark under the group that has nine cubes.

4 Trace the number. Draw to represent the number. Say the number.

5 Draw to show the addition word problem. Write an equation to model the problem. *There is one bird in the nest. Then two more birds fly into the nest. How many birds are in the nest now?*

Name _____

Represent 10

8   10

_____

- - - - - - - - - - -

_____

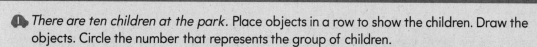

1. *There are ten children at the park.* Place objects in a row to show the children. Draw the objects. Circle the number that represents the group of children.
2. Count the stuffed bears in each group. Circle the group that has ten bears.
3. *Mavi has ten marbles.* Draw to represent the marbles. Write the number that represents the group of marbles.

Test Prep

 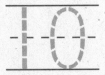

Spiral Review

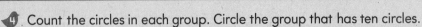

_____ ◯ _____ ◯ _____

4. Count the circles in each group. Circle the group that has ten circles.

5. Trace the number. Draw to represent the number. Say the number.

6. Listen to the story as you look at the picture. Write the equation to model how the group is being taken apart. *Andy has five tickets. Two tickets are for a movie on Saturday. The rest are for a movie on Sunday. How many tickets are for the Sunday movie?*

Name _____

Count and Write 6 and 7

 1

_____
- - - - - - -
_____

 2

_____
- - - - - - -
_____

 3
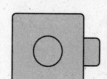

_____
- - - - - - -
_____

© Houghton Mifflin Harcourt Publishing Company

1–**2** Count the objects. Write the number.
3 *Kathleen has four cubes. How many more cubes does she need to have six cubes?*
Draw the cubes. Write the number to show the total number of cubes.

Module 8 • Lesson 1

seventy-five **P75**

Test Prep

5	6	7
○	○	○

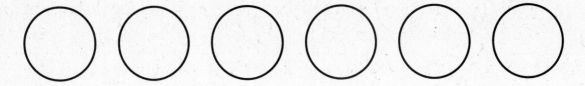

5	6	8
○	○	○

Spiral Review

___ ___ ___ is ___

© Houghton Mifflin Harcourt Publishing Company

4 – 5 Mark under the number that shows how many objects.

6 Listen to the subtraction word problem. Mark an X to show the objects being taken from the group. Write and trace the number sentence to model the problem. *Han has five star stickers in his pocket. He gives two stickers to his sister. How many star stickers are still in Han's pocket?*

Name _____

Count and Write 8 and 9

 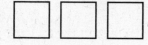

□ □ □
□ □
□ □
□ □

□ □ □ □
□ □ □ □

_____
- - - - - - -
_____

_____
- - - - - - -
_____

_____
- - - - - - -
_____

– Count the objects. Write the number.

Test Prep

7	8	9
○	○	○

_____   _____

- - - - -   - - - - -

_____   _____

Spiral Review

   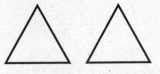

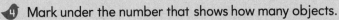

---

4 Mark under the number that shows how many objects.

5 Count the stars in each group. Write the number. Circle the group that has eight.

6 Listen to the addition word problem. Write an equation to model the problem. *Addie has two shapes. Then she finds two more shapes. How many shapes does Addie have now?*

Name _____

Count and Write 10

_____   _____

- - - - -   - - - - -

_____   _____

_____

- - - - -

_____ apples

---

① Count the stars. Write the numbers. Circle the group that shows 10.
② Count and circle ten apples. Write the number.

Test Prep

6   9   10

○   ○   ○

_____
— — — —
_____

Spiral Review

_____ _____ _____

© Houghton Mifflin Harcourt Publishing Company

3. Mark under the number that shows how many shirts.

4. Count the party hats. Write the number.

5. Listen to the subtraction word problem. Use objects or drawings to represent the problem.
Write the equation to model the problem. *There are five flowers in Joe's garden.*
Joe picks two of the flowers. How many flowers are still in the garden?

Name _____

Count and Order to 10

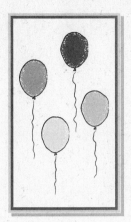  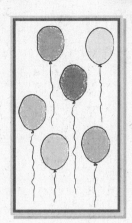 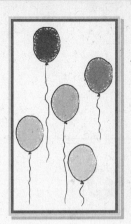

_____   _____   _____   _____

_____   _____   _____   _____

1 2 3 4 5 6 7 8 9 10

---

1. Count the balloons in each picture. Write the numbers as you count. Then write the numbers in counting order.

2. *Children are standing in a line. Will is number 5. Tyrone is number 7. Victoria is after Will and before Tyrone. If the children are in order by number, what number would Victoria be? Circle Victoria's number.*

Test Prep

 3

8, 6, 7, 10, 9   7, 9, 8, 6, 10   6, 7, 8, 9, 10
○   ○   ○

 4

| 4 | 5 | | | | |

Spiral Review

 5

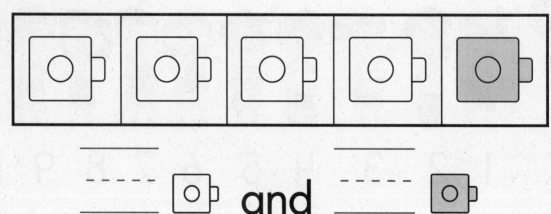

_ _ _ _ ⬜ and _ _ _ _ ⬜

© Houghton Mifflin Harcourt Publishing Company

3 Mark under the group of numbers that shows 6 to 10 in counting order.
4 Write the numbers in counting order. Say the numbers.
5 Write the numbers to represent the cubes in the five frame. Say the numbers that make 5.

© Houghton Mifflin Harcourt Publishing Company

Count to 100 by Ones

1	2	3	4	5	6	7	8	9	10
11	12	13	14	15	16	17	18	19	20
21	22	23	24	25	26	27	28	29	30
31	32	33	34	35	36	37	38	39	40
41	42	43	44	45	46	47	48	49	50

2

1	2	3	4	5	6	7	8	9	10
11	12	13	14	15	16	17	18	19	20
21	22	23	24	25	26	27	28	29	30

1 Look at the numbers in the shaded column. Use yellow to color the next column in the chart. How are the numbers in the yellow column the same as the numbers in the shaded column? How are they different? Begin at 1 and count by ones. Circle the number 14.

2 Look at the numbers in the shaded row. Use orange to color another row in the chart. How are the numbers in the orange row the same as the numbers in the shaded row? How are they different? Begin at 1 and count by ones. Circle the number 29.

Test Prep

1	2	3	4	5	6	7	8	9	10
11	12	13	14	15	16	17	18	19	20
21	22	23	24	25	26	27	28	29	30

5   10   16
○   ○   ○

1	2	3	4	5	6	7	8	9	10
11	12	13	14	15	16	17	18	19	20
21	22	23	24	25	26	27	28	29	30

1   6   10
○   ○   ○

Spiral Review

_____   _____

© Houghton Mifflin Harcourt Publishing Company

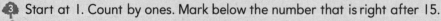

3. Start at 1. Count by ones. Mark below the number that is right after 15.

4. Start at 1. Count by ones. Mark below the number that is right after 5.

5. Look at the categories of color. Classify the cubes by the category of color. Write the total number of cubes in each category. *Nala has five cubes. She classifies the cubes by the category of color. How many cubes does Nala have of each color?*

LESSON 9.2
**More Practice/
Homework**

ONLINE
Video Tutorials and
Interactive Examples

Name

Count to 100 by Tens

1	2	3	4	5	6	7	8	9	10
11	12	13	14	15	16	17	18	19	20
21	22	23	24	25	26	27	28	29	30
31	32	33	34	35	36	37	38	39	40
41	42	43	44	45	46	47	48	49	50
51	52	53	54	55	56	57	58	59	60
61	62	63	64	65	66	67	68	69	70
71	72	73	74	75	76	77	78	79	80
81	82	83	84	85	86	87	88	89	90
91	92	93	94	95	96	97	98	99	100

1 Use yellow to color the number 10. Count to 100 by tens. Color each number as you count.

Test Prep

 2

1	2	3	4	5	6	7	8	9	10
11	12	13	14	15	16	17	18	19	20
21	22	23	24	25	26	27	28	29	30
31	32	33	34	35	36	37	38	39	40

20 ○   30 ○   40 ○

3

1	2	3	4	5	6	7	8	9	10
11	12	13	14	15	16	17	18	19	20
21	22	23	24	25	26	27	28	29	30
31	32	33	34	35	36	37	38	39	40
41	42	43	44	45	46	47	48	49	50

10 ○   30 ○   50 ○

Spiral Review

4   _____

---

2 Start at 10. Count by tens. Mark below the number that you count after 30.

3 Start at 10. Count by tens. Mark below the number that you count after 40.

4 *Tessa has two marbles. James gives Tessa three more marbles. How many marbles does Tessa have now? Write the total.*

LESSON 9.3
**More Practice/
Homework**

ONLINE
Video Tutorials and
Interactive Examples

Count Forward from a Given Number

---

1. There are 25 shells in the bucket. Beginning at 25, count forward. Mark an X on each shell as you count. Tell how many total shells there are.
2. There are 34 spoons in the container. Beginning at 34, count forward. Mark an X on each spoon as you count. Tell how many total spoons there are.

Test Prep

29	30	32
○	○	○

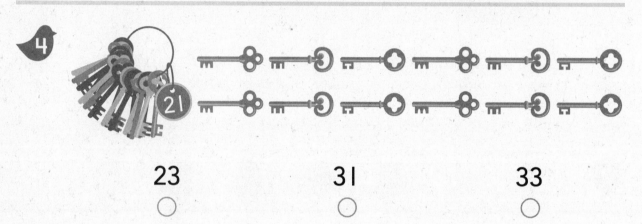

23	31	33
○	○	○

Spiral Review

_____   _____

🌳 There are 15 cars in the box. Beginning at 15, count forward. Mark an X on each car as you count. Mark below the number that tells how many total cars there are.

🐦 There are 21 keys on the ring. Beginning at 21, count forward. Mark an X on each key as you count. Mark below the number that tells how many total keys there are.

🌼 Count the objects in each group. Write the numbers. Compare the numbers. Circle the number that is greater.

Name _____

Identify a Greater Number of Objects Within 10

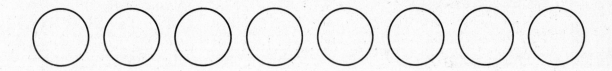

1. There are two groups of balloons. Draw lines to match the objects in each group. Circle the group that has a number of objects greater than the other group.

2. Draw lines to match the objects in each group. Circle the group that has a number of objects greater than the other group.

Test Prep

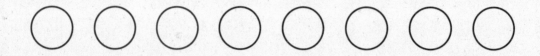

Spiral Review

_____ ◯ _____ ◯ _____

3. Draw lines to match the objects in each group. Circle the group that has a number of objects greater than the other group.

4. Draw lines to match the objects in each group. Circle the group that has a number of objects greater than the other group.

5. Look at the picture. Listen to the addition word problem. Write an equation to model the problem. _There are three ducks. One more duck joins them. How many ducks are there now?_

Name _____

Identify a Lesser Number of Objects Within 10

1

2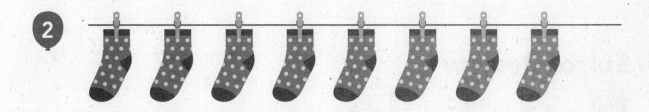

1 Draw lines to match the hats in each group. Circle the group that has a lesser number of hats.

2 Draw lines to match the objects in each group. Circle the group that has a number of objects less than the other group.

Test Prep

Spiral Review

3. There are two groups of marbles. Draw lines to match the objects in each group. Circle the group that has a number of objects less than the other group.

4. Draw lines to match the objects in each group. Circle the group that has a number of objects less than the other group.

5. Compare the group of books about birds with the group of books about tigers. Circle the group that has a number of books less than the other number of books.

Name _____

Match Equal Groups of Objects Within 10

2

3

1 Draw lines to match the objects in each group. Tell how you can identify whether the number of objects in one group is equal to the number of objects in the other group.

2 – 3 A store has groups of fruit. Draw lines to match the objects in each group. Circle the groups that show equal objects.

Test Prep

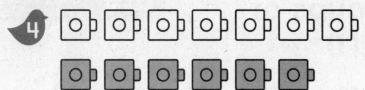 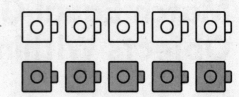

    Yes

   No

---

Spiral Review

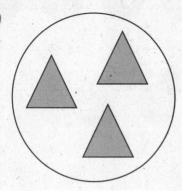 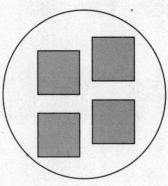 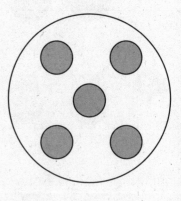

_____   _____   _____

---

4 Circle the groups that show equal objects.

5 Draw lines to match the counters in each group. Are the groups equal? Circle Yes or No.

6 The groups are sorted by shape. Write the number of shapes in each group.

Name _____

Compare Groups Within 10 by Counting

 1

_____

_____

2

_____

_____

---

1 Compare the fruits in each group by counting. Write the number of fruits in each group. Circle the number that is less.

2 Count the number of children in each group. Write the number. Circle the number that is greater.

Test Prep

 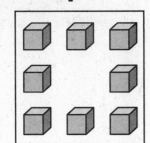   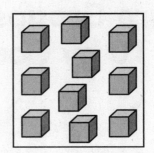

_____   _____

    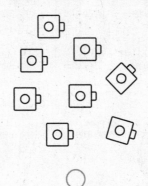   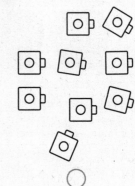

◯   ◯   ◯

Spiral Review

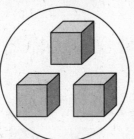   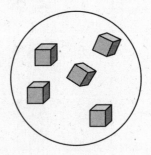

Big _____   Small _____

3 Compare the blocks in each group by counting. Write the number of blocks. Circle the number that is greater.

4 *Fran has some gray cubes. Ben has the same number of white cubes.* Mark below the group that shows Ben's cubes.

5 The groups of blocks are sorted by size. Write the number of blocks in each group.

Name _____

Compare Groups Within 10 by Matching

1 _____

_____

2

_____

_____

1 Listen to the story. How can you represent and compare the bags by matching? Write the number for each group. *Ana tosses nine bean bags. Meg tosses less bean bags than Ana.* Write the number of bean bags in each group.

2 Listen to the story. Draw to show a number of vases Max could have. Draw lines to match the objects in each group. Write the number of objects in each group. *Max has six flowers. He has more vases than he has flowers.*

Test Prep

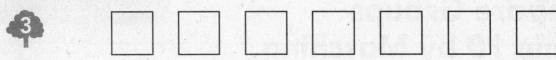

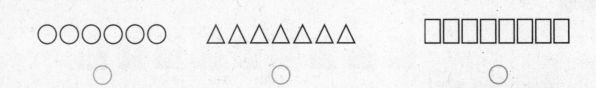

Spiral Review

3. Casey draws seven squares. Then she draws a group of other shapes that has more objects than the group of squares. Mark under the group of objects that could be the shapes Casey draws.

4. There are eight counters in a group. There is another group of counters that has less objects than the group of eight counters. Mark under the group of counters that could be this group.

5. Count the number of cubes. Draw and match to show an equal number of objects.

LESSON 10.6
**More Practice/
Homework**

⊙Ed **ONLINE**
Video Tutorials and
Interactive Examples

Name _____

Compare Numbers Within 10

 1 8

_____

2 5

_____

 3 9

_____

4

1	2	3	4
5	6	7	8

9	10

_____

_____

© Houghton Mifflin Harcourt Publishing Company

1 Write a number within ten that is less than the number shown.
2 Write a number within ten that is greater than the number shown.
3 Write a number within ten that is less than the number shown.
4 Choose two different numbers within ten. Write the numbers. Circle the greater number.

Test Prep

 3   7

---

 6   8   10
                     ○   ○   ○

Spiral Review

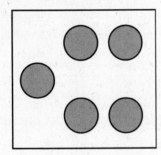   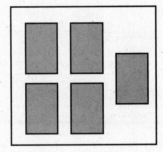   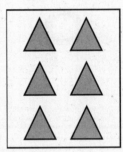

_____   _____   _____

5	
6	

© Houghton Mifflin Harcourt Publishing Company

5 Circle the lesser number.
6 Mark below the number that is greater than nine.
7 Write the number in each category. Sort the categories by count.

Name _____

Act Out Addition Problems Within 10

_____ ◯ _____ ◯ _____

_____ ◯ _____ ◯ _____

_____ ◯ _____ ◯ _____

1. Listen to the addition word problem. Act out and draw a quick picture to represent the problem. Write the equation to model the problem. *There are seven birds. Three more birds join them. How many birds are there now?*

2. Act out and tell an addition word problem to match the picture. Write the equation to model the problem.

3. Listen to the addition word problem. How can you act out and draw quick pictures to represent the problem? Write the equation to model the problem. *Manuel picks six apples. He picks two more. How many apples does Manuel pick?*

Test Prep

$1 + 5 = 6$ $2 + 4 = 6$ $3 + 4 = 7$
   ○   ○   ○

_____ ◯ _____ ◯ _____

Spiral Review

1	2	3	4	5	6	7	8	9	10
11	12	13	14	15	16	17	18	19	20
21	22	23	24	25	26	27	28	29	30

4. Listen to the addition word problem. Mark under the equation that models the problem. *There are two fish. Four more fish join them. How many fish are swimming now?*

5. Listen to the addition word problem. Write the equation to model the problem. *Three birds are in a tree. Five more birds join them. How many birds are in the tree now?*

6. Begin at 1 and count. Circle the number 26.

Name _____

Act Out Subtraction Problems Within 10

_____ ◯ _____ ◯ _____

_____ ◯ _____ ◯ _____

_____ ◯ _____ ◯ _____

 Listen to the subtraction word problem. Act out and draw a quick picture to represent the problem. Write the equation to model the problem. *There are nine deer in the field. Four of the deer leave. How many deer are in the field now?*

2 Act out and tell a subtraction word problem to match the picture. Write the equation to model the problem.

3 Listen to the subtraction word problem. How can you act out and draw quick pictures to represent the problem? Write the equation to model the problem. *Ten acorns are on the ground. A squirrel takes three of the acorns. How many acorns are on the ground now?*

Test Prep

$6 - 2 = 4$ $8 - 2 = 6$ $9 - 3 = 6$

_____ ◯ _____ ◯ _____

Spiral Review

 ☆ ☆ ☆ ☆ ☆ ☆ ☆ ☆

☆ ☆ ☆ ☆ ☆ ☆ ☆ ☆ ☆ ☆

Listen to the subtraction word problem. Mark under the equation that models the problem. *There are eight leaves on the ground. Maura picks up two of the leaves. How many leaves are on the ground now?*

Listen to the subtraction word problem. Draw a quick picture to represent the problem. Write the equation to model the problem. *There are seven birds on a wire. Six of the birds fly away. How many birds are still on the wire?*

Count the stars in each group. Circle the group that has eight stars.

Name _____

LESSON 11.3
More Practice/ Homework

ONLINE
Video Tutorials and
Interactive Examples

Solve Add To Problems Within 10

_____ ◯ _____ ◯ _____

2

_____ ◯ _____ ◯ _____

3

_____ ◯ _____ ◯ _____

① Listen to the addition word problem. How can you use objects or drawings to represent and solve the problem? Write the equation to model how to add to a group. *There are two rabbits in the field. Four more rabbits hop into the field. How many rabbits are in the field now?*

② Think of a group of balloons. How can more balloons be added to the group? Tell an addition word problem about adding to a group using numbers within 10. Draw to represent and solve the problem. Write the equation to model the problem.

③ Listen to the addition word problem. Write the equation to model the problem. Solve the problem. *There are seven ladybugs in a group. Two more ladybugs join them. How many ladybugs are in the group now?*

Test Prep

$$6 + 2 = 8 \qquad 5 + 3 = 8 \qquad 4 + 2 = 6$$

◯ ◯ ◯

_____ ◯ _____ ◯ _____

Spiral Review

5	6			

---

4 Listen to the addition word problem. Mark under the addition equation that models the problem. *There are six squirrels. Two more squirrels join them. How many squirrels are there now?*

5 Listen to the addition word problem. Write the equation to model the problem. Solve the problem. *There are four canoes in the pond. Then three kayaks are put in the pond. How many boats are in the pond now?*

6 Write the numbers in counting order. Say the numbers.

Name _____

Solve Take From Problems Within 10

 1

2

 3

---

1 Listen to the subtraction word problem. How can you use objects or drawings to represent and solve the problem? Write the equation to model how to take from a group. *Eight children are at the park. Three children leave. How many children are still at the park?*

2 Think of a group of apples, and some of the apples get eaten. Tell a subtraction word problem about taking from a group using numbers within 10. Use drawings to represent and solve the problem. Write the equation to model the problem.

3 Listen to the subtraction word problem. Use objects or drawings to represent and solve the problem. Write the equation to model the problem. *There are nine dragonflies in a field. Five dragonflies fly away. How many dragonflies are in the field now?*

Test Prep

$6 - 3 = 3$ $8 - 3 = 5$ $9 - 3 = 6$

◯   ◯   ◯

____ ____ ____

Spiral Review

    3   4

    2   1

    5   3

© Houghton Mifflin Harcourt Publishing Company

4. Listen to the subtraction word problem. Mark under the subtraction equation that models the problem. *There are nine squirrels. Three squirrels leave. How many squirrels are there now?*

5. Listen to the subtraction word problem. Write the equation to model the problem. *Six children are talking. Three children leave. How many children are still talking?*

6 – 8 Circle the greater number.

Name _____

LESSON 11.5
More Practice/ Homework

ONLINE
Video Tutorials and
Interactive Examples

Write Addition Equations Within 10

1

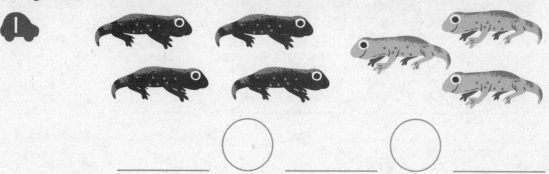

_____ ◯ _____ ◯ _____

2

◯ ◯

_____ _____ _____

3

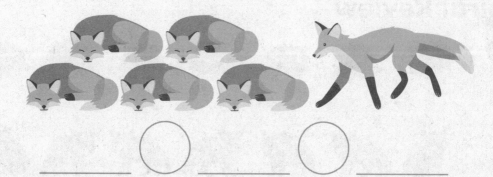

◯ ◯

_____ _____ _____

---

1 Listen to the addition word problem. Write an equation to model the problem. Explain what each number represents. *Four lizards are resting. Three more lizards join them. How many lizards are there now?*

2 Think of a group of animals, and more animals joining them. Tell an addition word problem about adding to a group using numbers within 10. Draw to represent and solve the problem. Write an equation to model the problem.

3 Look at the picture. Tell an addition word problem about the foxes in the picture. Write an equation to model the problem. Explain what each number represents.

Test Prep

_____ ◯ _____ ◯ _____

_____ ◯ _____ ◯ _____

Spiral Review

4 Listen to the addition word problem. Write an equation to model the problem. *Seven ducks are swimming on a pond. Two more ducks join them. How many ducks are on the pond now?*

5 Look at the picture. Write an addition equation to model the picture.

6 Circle the group that has a number of animals greater than the other group.

Name _____

Write Subtraction Equations Within 10

1

____ ◯ ____ ◯ ____

2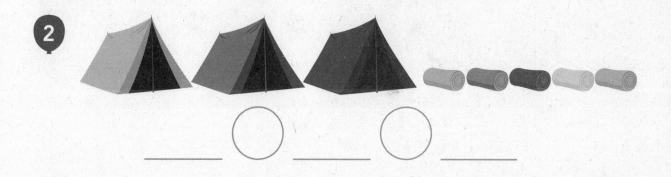

____ ◯ ____ ◯ ____

3

____ ◯ ____ ◯ ____

Listen to the subtraction word problem in Problems 1 and 2. Mark an X to represent taking from the group. Write an equation to model the problem. Explain what each number represents.

1 *Seven deer are in a field. Some of the deer leave to go into the forest. How many deer are in the field now?*

2 *There are eight tents set up at a campground. People take down and roll up five of the tents. How many of the tents have not been taken down?*

3 *Think of a group of animals and some of the animals are leaving. Tell a subtraction word problem about taking from a group using numbers within 10. Draw to represent and solve the problem. Write the equation to model the problem.*

Test Prep

$$7 - 5 = 2 \qquad 6 - 4 = 2 \qquad 6 - 3 = 3$$

◯　　　　　◯　　　　　◯

_____ ◯ _____ ◯ _____

Spiral Review

_____ ◯ _____ ◯ _____

---

4. Look at the picture. Mark under the equation that models owls leaving the branch.
5. Look at the picture. Write an equation to model the problem.
6. Listen to the subtraction word problem as you look at the picture. How can you solve the problem? Write the equation. *There are five dogs. Three of the dogs have pointy ears. The rest of the dogs have floppy ears. How many dogs have floppy ears?*

Name _____

LESSON 11.7
More Practice/ Homework

ONLINE
Video Tutorials and
Interactive Examples

Solve Result Unknown Word Problems Within 10

1

_____ ◯ _____ ◯ _____

2

_____ ◯ _____ ◯ _____

1. Think of a group of animals, and more animals joining them. Tell an addition word problem about adding to a group using numbers within 10. Draw to represent and solve the problem. Write an equation to model the problem.

2. Look at the picture. Tell a subtraction word problem about the frogs. Mark an X on the frogs that leave. How many are still in the pond? Write an equation to model the problem.

Test Prep

 3

7 + 2 = 9   6 + 3 = 9   6 + 2 = 8

○   ○   ○

Spiral Review

 4

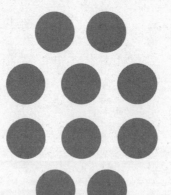

3 Look at the picture. Mark under the equation that models the chipmunks joining the group.

4 Count the shapes in each group. Circle the groups that have ten shapes.

Name _____

Represent Addition Problems Within 10 Using Objects and Drawings

 1

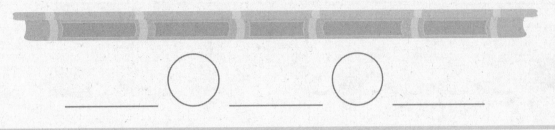

_____ ◯ _____ ◯ _____

 2

_____ ◯ _____ ◯ _____

 3

_____ ◯ _____ ◯ _____

1. Listen to the addition word problem. How can you represent the problem using objects or drawings? Write the equation to model the problem. *There are four daisies and three tulips in the flower box. How many flowers are in the flower box?*

Listen to the addition word problem. Draw quick pictures to represent the problem. Write the equation to model the problem.

2. *Taylor has seven gray books and three white books. How many books does she have?*

3. *Tori has two blue marbles. She also has four yellow marbles. How many marbles does Tori have?*

Test Prep

_____ ◯ _____ ◯ _____

$4 + 4 = 8$ $5 + 4 = 9$ $7 + 2 = 9$

◯   ◯   ◯

Spiral Review

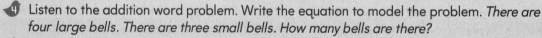

_____

 Listen to the addition word problem. Write the equation to model the problem. *There are four large bells. There are three small bells. How many bells are there?*

Listen to the addition word problem. Mark under the equation that models the problem. *Pablo sees five dragonflies in the field. He also sees four crickets in the field. How many insects does Pablo see?*

Listen to the word problem. Draw to represent the problem. Write the answer to the question in the problem. *The bookshelf has one red book and two blue books. How many books are on the shelf?*

Name _____

LESSON 12.2
More Practice/ Homework

ONLINE
Video Tutorials and
Interactive Examples

Represent Subtraction Problems Within 10 Using Objects and Drawings

_____ ◯ _____ ◯ _____

2

_____ ◯ _____ ◯ _____

---

1 Listen to the subtraction word problem. How can you represent the problem using objects or drawings? Write the equation to model the problem. *There are seven chairs on the porch. Four are rocking chairs. How many are not rocking chairs?*

2 Listen to the subtraction word problem. Draw quick pictures to represent the problem. Write the equation to model the problem. *There are six crayons on the desk. Two of the crayons are red. The rest are blue. How many crayons are blue?*

Test Prep

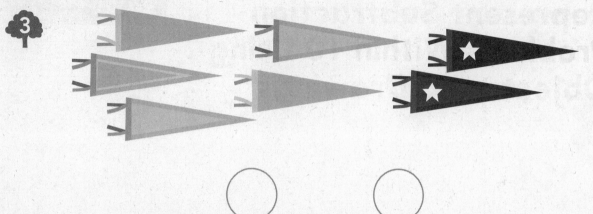

⌇ 3

( )   ( )

____   ○   ____   ○   ____

🐦 4

$10 - 3 = 7$ $7 - 3 = 4$ $8 - 3 = 5$

○   ○   ○

Spiral Review

_____

🌳 3 Listen to the subtraction word problem. Write the equation to model the problem. *There are seven pennants. Two have stars on them. The rest do not have stars. How many pennants do not have stars?*

🐦 4 Listen to the subtraction word problem. Mark under the equation that models the problem. *There are eight mugs on the table. Three mugs have a flower on them. The rest do not have a flower. How many mugs do not have a flower?*

✹ 5 Listen to the word problem. Write the answer to the question in the problem. *There are four cans on the shelf. Two cans contain fruit. The rest of the cans contain soup. How many cans contain soup?*

Name _____

LESSON 12.3
More Practice/ Homework

ONLINE
Video Tutorials and
Interactive Examples

Solve Put Together Problems Within 10

1

_____ ◯ _____ ◯ _____

2

_____ ◯ _____ ◯ _____

3

_____ ◯ _____ ◯ _____

Listen to the word problem as you look at the picture. Write the equation to model how many in each group are put together. Solve the problem.

1 *There are three open umbrellas and three closed umbrellas. How many umbrellas are there?*

2 *Four rain hats and five raincoats are on the coat rack. How many objects are on the coat rack?*

3 *Joel sees some shirts in the store window. Five shirts have flowers and two shirts have stripes. How many shirts does Joel see in the store window?*

Test Prep

$$2 + 4 = 6 \qquad\qquad 2 + 6 = 8 \qquad\qquad 6 - 2 = 4$$

◯   ◯   ◯

_____ ◯ _____ ◯ _____

Spiral Review

4. Mark under the equation that models how many scarves and sunglasses are on the store shelf.

5. Listen to the addition word problem. Solve the problem. Write the equation to model the problem. *There are two books with smiley faces on the cover and eight books with stars on the cover. How many books are there?*

6. Compare the number of airplanes with the number of helicopters. Circle the group that has a number of objects that is less than the other group.

Name _____

Solve Take Apart Problems Within 10

_____ _____ ◯ _____ ◯ _____

_____ _____ ◯ _____ ◯ _____

_____ _____ ◯ _____ ◯ _____

_____ _____ ◯ _____ ◯ _____

Listen to the word problem. How can you use objects or drawings to represent and solve the problem? Write the equation to model how the groups are taken apart.

1. *There are seven children in the classroom. Four children are sitting in chairs. The rest are standing. How many children are standing?*

Listen to the word problem as you look at the picture. Write the equation to model how the group is being taken apart. Solve the problem.

2. *There are eight children on the beach. Four children are playing ball. The rest are playing in the sand. How many children are playing in the sand?*

3. *There are ten birds on the beach. Five birds are big. The rest are small. How many birds are small?*

Test Prep

$$7 - 6 = 1 \qquad 7 - 5 = 2 \qquad 6 - 1 = 5$$

   ○

_____ ○ _____ ○ _____

Spiral Review

_____

 Listen to the word problem. Mark under the equation that models how the group is being taken apart. *Seven children are playing soccer. Five children are on the field. The rest are sitting on the bench. How many children are sitting on the bench?*

Listen to the word problem. Write the equation to model how the group is being taken apart. Solve the problem. *Six buses are at the school. Three of the buses have stripes. The rest of the buses do not have stripes. How many buses do not have stripes?*

Count the cats. Write the number.

Solve Word Problems Within 10

Listen to the word problem. Draw to represent and solve the problem. Write the equation to model the problem.

1. *There are six baseballs and two footballs. How many sports balls are there?*

2. *There are seven plates. Three plates are yellow and the rest are red. How many plates are red?*

© Houghton Mifflin Harcourt Publishing Company

Test Prep

$$2 + 4 = 6 \qquad 3 + 5 = 8 \qquad 5 - 3 = 2$$

○   ○   ○

_____ ○ _____ ○ _____

Spiral Review

_____   _____

🌳 **3** Mark under the equation that matches the problem. *Three apples and five oranges are on the table. How many pieces of fruit are on the table?*

🐦 **4** Listen to the word problem. Solve the problem. Write the equation to model the problem. *Kaya has eight stickers. Two of the stickers are bears. The rest are stars. How many star stickers does Kaya have?*

✦ **5** Count and write the number of bears in each group. Circle the number that is greater.

LESSON 13.1
**More Practice/
Homework**

ONLINE
Ed
Video Tutorials and
Interactive Examples

Ways to Make 6 and 7

$$6 = \underline{\quad} + \underline{\quad}$$

$$6 = \underline{\quad} + \underline{\quad}$$

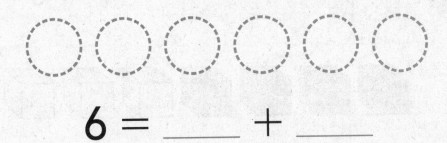

$$7 = \underline{\quad} + \underline{\quad}$$

$$7 = \underline{\quad} + \underline{\quad}$$

Listen to the story. Color the objects to show different ways to make the number. For each way, complete the equation.

1 *Julie sees six balloons. Some balloons are blue and some are yellow. How many balloons of each color might she see?*

2 *Emma picks seven apples. Some apples are red and some are green. How many of each color apple might Emma pick?*

Test Prep

3   • 6 = 2 + 4

   • 6 = 1 + 5

   • 6 = 4 + 2

   • 6 = 3 + 3

 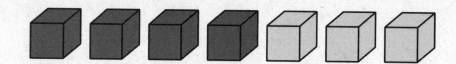

     7 = 4 + 3   7 = 5 + 2   7 = 6 + 1

Spiral Review

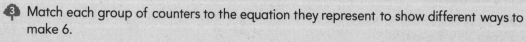

3   Match each group of counters to the equation they represent to show different ways to make 6.

4   Mark below the equation that shows the way to make 7 that is represented by the cubes.

5   Draw to represent the number. Say the number.

© Houghton Mifflin Harcourt Publishing Company

LESSON 13.2
**More Practice/
Homework**

ONLINE
Video Tutorials and
Interactive Examples

Ways to Make 8

$$8 = \underline{\qquad} + \underline{\qquad}$$

$$8 = \underline{\qquad} + \underline{\qquad}$$

$$\underline{\qquad} + \underline{\qquad} = 8$$

$$8 = \underline{\qquad} + \underline{\qquad}$$

Listen to the story. Color the cubes to show different ways to make 8. For each way, complete the equation. *Michael loves to read. He has eight books. Some of Michael's books are about dragons and some are about whales. How many of each type of book might Michael have?*

Test Prep

2

$$8 = \underline{\hspace{1cm}} + \underline{\hspace{1cm}}$$

3

$8 = 4 + 4$ $\quad\quad 8 = 5 + 3$ ○ $\quad\quad 8 = 6 + 2$ ○

Spiral Review

4

$$\underline{\hspace{1.5cm}} \bigcirc \underline{\hspace{1.5cm}} \bigcirc \underline{\hspace{1.5cm}}$$

---

2 The counters show one way to make 8. Complete the equation to match the counters.

3 Mark below the equation that shows the way to make 8 that is represented by the leaves.

4 Listen to the addition word problem. Use objects or drawings to represent the problem. Complete the equation to model the problem. *There are five children reading in a group. Two more children join them. How many children are now reading in the group?*

LESSON 13.3
**More Practice/
Homework**

ONLINE
Video Tutorials and
Interactive Examples

Name _____

Ways to Make 9

$$9 = \underline{} + \underline{}$$

$$\underline{} + \underline{} = 9$$

$$9 = \underline{} + \underline{}$$

$$9 = \underline{} + \underline{}$$

1. Listen to the story. Color the cubes to show different ways to make 9. For each way, complete the equation. *Maya sees nine bunnies in the park. Some of the bunnies are brown and some are white. How many bunnies of each color might she see?*

Test Prep

 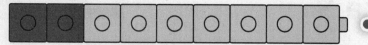

$9 = 5 + 4$

$9 = 6 + 3$

$9 = 2 + 7$

$9 = 8 + 1$

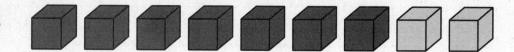

$9 = 6 + 3$ $9 = 7 + 2$ $9 = 8 + 1$

○   ○   ○

Spiral Review

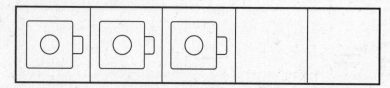

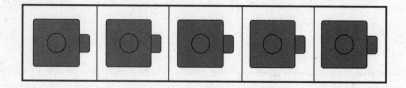

---

2 Match each group of cubes to the equation they represent to show different ways to make 9.

3 Mark below the equation that shows the way to make 9 that is represented by the cubes.

4 Compare the groups of white and gray cubes. Circle the group with the greater number of objects.

Name _____

LESSON 13.4
More Practice/ Homework

ONLINE
Video Tutorials and Interactive Examples

Ways to Make 10

$$10 = \underline{\quad} + \underline{\quad}$$

$$10 = \underline{\quad} + \underline{\quad}$$

$$10 = \underline{\quad} + \underline{\quad}$$

© Houghton Mifflin Harcourt Publishing Company

Listen to the story. Draw to show three ways to make 10. For each way, complete the equation. *Jin has ten pencils. He puts some pencils in the light gray box and some in the dark gray box. How many pencils might there be in each box?*

Module 13 • Lesson 4

one hundred thirty-one **P131**

Test Prep

2 🎈

10 = 2 + 8

10 = 5 + 5

10 = 6 + 4

10 = 3 + 7

10 = 9 + 1

3 🌳

$$10 = \underline{\hphantom{000}} + \underline{\hphantom{000}}$$

Spiral Review

$$\underline{\hphantom{000}} + \underline{\hphantom{000}} = \underline{\hphantom{000}}$$

---

2 Match each group of cubes to the equation they represent to show different ways to make 10.

3 The balloons show one way to make 10. Complete the equation to match the balloons.

4 Listen to the story. Use objects and drawings to represent the addition word problem. Write the equation. *There are three children eating at a table. One more child joins them. How many children are eating at the table now?*

Make 10 from a Given Number

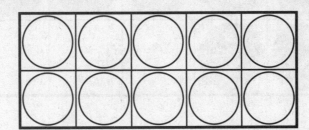

$$6 \; + \; \underline{\hspace{2cm}} \; = \; \underline{\hspace{2cm}}$$

$$5 \; + \; \underline{\hspace{2cm}} \; = \; \underline{\hspace{2cm}}$$

$$2 \; + \; \underline{\hspace{2cm}} \; = \; \underline{\hspace{2cm}}$$

Listen to the story. Color or draw to make 10. Complete the equation.

1. Rosita has ten counters. Six of the counters are red. The rest are yellow. How many counters are yellow?

2. Sebastian wants to make ten cards to send to his friends. He has made five cards so far. How many more cards does Sebastian need to make?

3. Dylan needs ten plates for the picnic. She has two plates. How many more plates does she need?

Test Prep

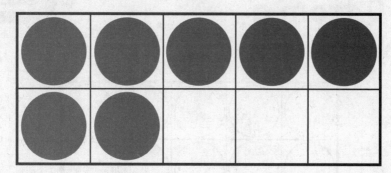

$$7 \quad + \underline{\hspace{2cm}} = \underline{\hspace{2cm}}$$

$$9 \quad + \underline{\hspace{2cm}} = \underline{\hspace{2cm}}$$

Spiral Review

      4   2

---

      3   5

---

4   Listen to the story. Draw to make 10. Complete the equation. *Pierre has ten counters. Seven of the counters are gray. The rest are white. How many counters are white?*

5   Listen to the story. Draw to make 10. Complete the equation. *Nala needs ten buttons. She has nine buttons. How many more buttons does she need?*

6   Look at the numbers. Think about the counting order. Circle the number that is less.

7   Look at the numbers. Think about the counting order. Circle the number that is greater.

Name _____

LESSON 14.1
**More Practice/
Homework**

 ONLINE
Video Tutorials and
Interactive Examples

Identify and Describe Spheres

  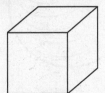  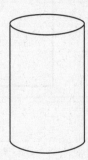

  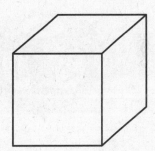

1. Circle the sphere.
2. Color the shape with a curved surface.
3. Mark an X on the object that has only a curved surface.

Module 14 • Lesson 1   one hundred thirty-five **P135**

Test Prep

 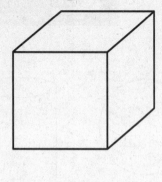  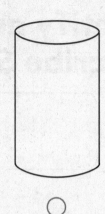

○   ○   ○

Spiral Review

_____ ◯ _____ ◯ _____

© Houghton Mifflin Harcourt Publishing Company

---

4   Mark below the sphere.

5   Mark an X on the object with a curved surface.

6   Listen to the subtraction word problem. Write the equation to model how the group is being taken apart. *There are four birds flying. Three of the birds are gray. The rest are black. How many birds are black?*

LESSON 14.2
**More Practice/
Homework**

 ONLINE
Video Tutorials and
Interactive Examples

Identify and Describe Cubes

   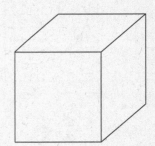

© Houghton Mifflin Harcourt Publishing Company

1. Color the cube.
2. Mark an X on the object that has only flat surfaces that are all the same size.
3. Mark an X on the objects that only have flat surfaces.

Test Prep

 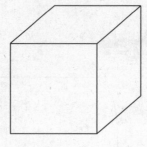 

◯   ◯   ◯

Spiral Review

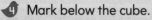
_____ ◯ _____ ◯ _____

© Houghton Mifflin Harcourt Publishing Company

4   Mark below the cube.

5   Mark an X on the object with all flat surfaces.

6   Listen to the addition word problem. Write the equation to show how many in each group
are put together. Solve the equation. *There are three big fish and two small fish. How many
fish are there?*

LESSON 14.3
**More Practice/
Homework**

ONLINE
Video Tutorials and
Interactive Examples

Identify and Describe Cylinders

1 Circle the cylinders.
2 Mark an X on the object that has a curved surface and two flat surfaces.
3 Mark an X on the object with two flat surfaces and a curved surface.

Test Prep

  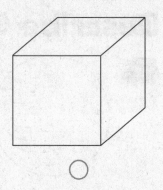

○ ○ ○

○ ○ ○

Spiral Review

61	62	63	64	65	66	67	68	69	70
71	72	73	74	75	76	77	78	79	80
81	82	83	84	85	86	87	88	89	90
91	92	93	94	95	96	97	98	99	100

4 Mark below the cylinder.

5 Mark below the object with two flat surfaces and a curved surface.

6 Find the number 78. Count forward to 100. Use yellow to color the numbers you count.

Name _____

Identify and Describe Cones

 1

 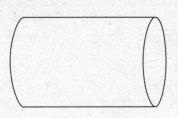 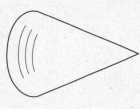 

2

 3

FOOD

---

1. Circle the cones.
2 Mark an X on the object that has one flat surface and a curved surface.
3 Circle the object with one flat surface and a curved surface.

Test Prep

○   ○   ○

○   ○   ○

Spiral Review

4 Mark below the cone.
5 Mark below the object with one flat surface and a curved surface.
6 Circle the group that has a number of objects less than the other group.

LESSON 14.5
**More Practice/
Homework**

ONLINE
Video Tutorials and
Interactive Examples

Build Shapes

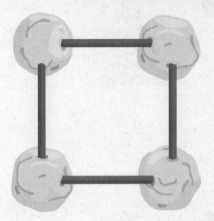

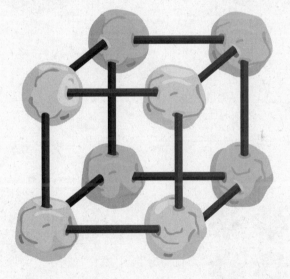

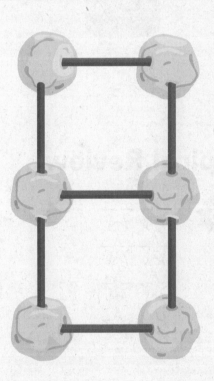

1 Circle the shape you can make if you connect four clay balls with sticks.
2 Circle the shape you can make if you connect eight clay balls with sticks.

Test Prep

 3

○   ○   ○

 4

○   ○   ○

Spiral Review

 5

3 Mark below the object that is shaped like a sphere.
4 Mark below the object that is shaped like a cube.
5 Count the objects in each group. Compare the groups. Circle the two groups that have the same number of objects.

LESSON 15.1
**More Practice/
Homework**

ONLINE
Video Tutorials and
Interactive Examples

Use *Above* and *Below*
to Describe Position

---

1 Circle the object that is shaped like a cube above the oatmeal.

2 Mark an X on the object that is shaped like a cylinder below the basketball.

3 Where are the cubes in the picture? Draw an object shaped like a sphere above an object shaped like a cube.

Test Prep

○   ○   ○

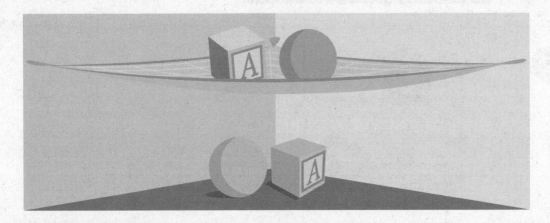

Spiral Review

$$8 = \underline{\hspace{1.5cm}} + \underline{\hspace{1.5cm}}$$

---

4 Mark below the picture that shows the object that is shaped like a sphere above the object that is shaped like a cone.

5 Mark an X on the object that is shaped like a cube below the net.

6 Listen to the story. Color the cubes to show a way to make 8. Complete the equation.
Meg has eight apples to make a pie. Some of the apples are red and some are green. How many of each color apple might there be?

Name _____

Use *Next To* and *Beside* to Describe Position

1

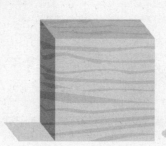

2

3

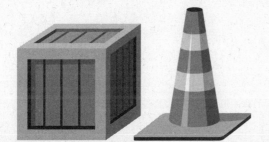

1 Circle the object that is shaped like a cube beside the marble.
2 Mark an X on the object that is shaped like a cylinder next to the child.
3 How would you describe where the traffic cone is in each picture? Circle the traffic cone that is beside the box.

Module 15 • Lesson 2

one hundred forty-seven **P147**

Test Prep

○   ○   ○

Spiral Review

 Mark an X on the object that is shaped like a cylinder beside the box of tea.

 Mark below the picture that shows the object that is shaped like a cube next to the object that is shaped like a sphere.

 Count the circles. Draw to show a group that has a greater number of circles. Draw lines to match the objects in each group.

Use *In Front Of* and *Behind* to Describe Position

1. Circle the object that is shaped like a cube in front of the globe.
2. Mark an X on the object that is shaped like a cube behind the cone.
3. How can you describe where the animals are? Circle the animal that is in front of the duck. Mark an X on the animal that is behind the rabbit.

Test Prep

○   ○   ○

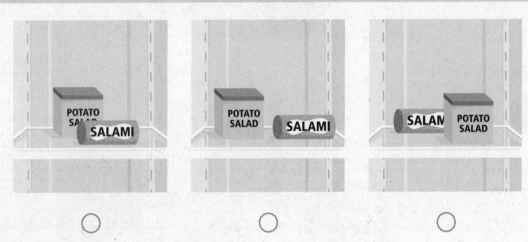

○   ○   ○

Spiral Review

_____

_____

4 Mark below the picture that shows the object that is shaped like a cube in front of the object that is shaped like a cylinder.

5 Mark below the picture that shows the object that is shaped like a cylinder behind the object that is shaped like a cube.

6 Count the number of stars in each group. Write the number. Circle the number that is greater.

Name _____

Identify and Describe Circles

 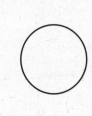

2

3

1 Mark an X on all the shapes with a curve.
2 Color the flat shapes.
3 Circle the object shaped like a circle.

Module 16 • Lesson 1

one hundred fifty-one **P151**

Test Prep

   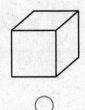

Spiral Review

___ ◯ ___ ◯ ___

4 Mark under the shape that is curved.
5 Mark an X on the circle.
6 Circle the shape that is flat.
7 Listen to the subtraction word problem. Use objects or drawings to represent the problem. Complete the equation to model the problem. *Six birds are in a tree. One bird flies away. How many birds are in the tree now?*

Name _____

Identify and Describe Squares

 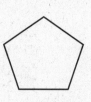 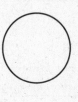 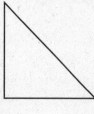

2

May						
Sunday	Monday	Tuesday	Wednesday	Thursday	Friday	Saturday
			1	2	3	4
5	6	7	8	9	10	11
12	13	14	15	16	17	18
19	20	21	22	23	24	25
26	27	28	29	30	31	

1 Mark an X on the squares.
2 Circle the object shaped like a square.
3 Draw the smallest square you can by connecting dots on the dot paper.

Test Prep

   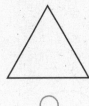

○   ○   ○

Spiral Review

_____ ◯ _____ ◯ _____

4   Mark under the shape that has four equal sides and four vertices.

5   Mark an X on the square.

6   Mark an X on the shape that is flat.

7   Listen to the word problem. Draw to represent the problem. Write an equation to model the problem. *Luis has nine grapes on his plate. Five of the grapes are purple and the rest of the grapes are green. How many green grapes are on the plate?*

© Houghton Mifflin Harcourt Publishing Company

P154   one hundred fifty-four

LESSON 16.3
**More Practice/
Homework**

Ed **ONLINE**
Video Tutorials and
Interactive Examples

Name _____

Identify and Describe Triangles

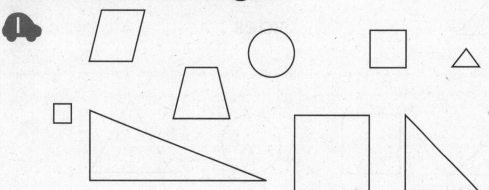

1. Mark an X on all the shapes with three sides and three vertices.
2. Color the flat shapes.
3. Draw three dots that are not in a row. Connect the dots. What shape did you make?

© Houghton Mifflin Harcourt Publishing Company

Test Prep

 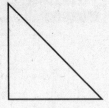
_____ sides

Spiral Review

   _____

4 Look at the shape. Write the number of sides.

5 Mark an X on the triangles.

6 Mark under the shape that is flat.

7 Listen to the addition word problem. Write the equation to model how many in each group are put together. Solve the equation. *Vanessa has three toy cars. Mario has three toy cars. How many toy cars are there?*

LESSON 16.4
**More Practice/
Homework**

ONLINE
Video Tutorials and
Interactive Examples

Name _____

Identify and Describe Rectangles

1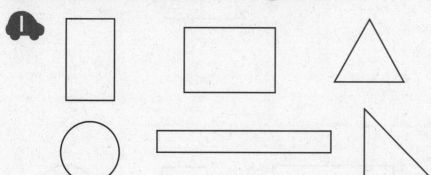

2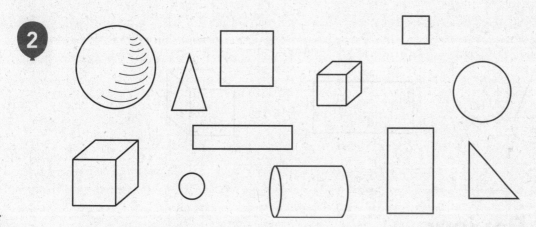

3

1 Mark an X on the shapes with four sides and four vertices.
2 Color the flat shapes.
3 Circle the object shaped like a rectangle.

Test Prep

 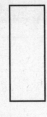

Spiral Review

 6   9

© Houghton Mifflin Harcourt Publishing Company

 Mark under the shape that has four sides.
 Mark an X on the rectangles.
Mark an X on the shape that is flat.
Look at the numbers. Compare the numbers. Circle the greater number.

Name _____

Identify and Describe Hexagons

 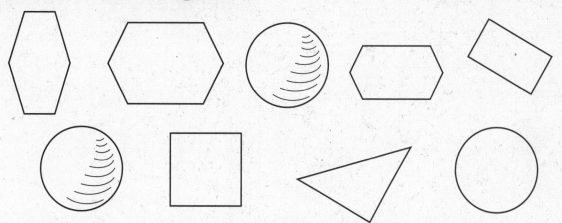

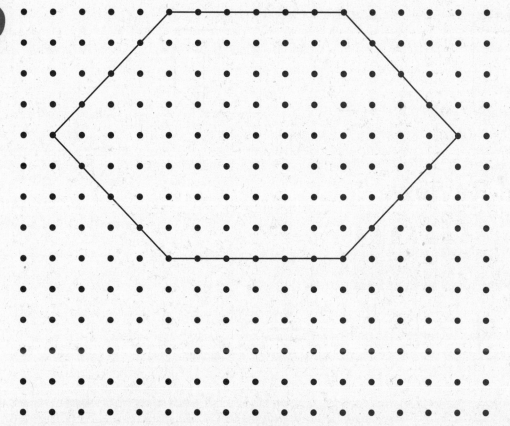

---

1. Mark an X on all the shapes with six sides and six vertices.
2. Draw a smaller hexagon than the one shown.

Test Prep

 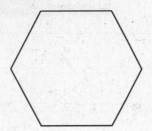 _____ vertices

  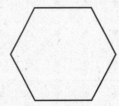 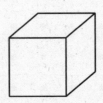

Spiral Review

$$4 + \underline{\quad} = \underline{\quad}$$

---

3 Circle each vertex. Write the number of vertices.
4 Mark under the hexagon.
5 Mark an X on the shape that is flat.
6 *Tina needs ten crayons. She has four crayons. How many more crayons does Tina need to make ten? Complete the equation.*

Compose Simple Shapes

  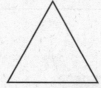 

---

1. Use smaller shapes to make this shape. Draw to show the shapes you used.
2. Use the two smaller shapes shown to form the larger shape. Color the shapes to show how you made the larger shape.
3. Draw to show a way you can use the squares to form a rectangle.

Test Prep

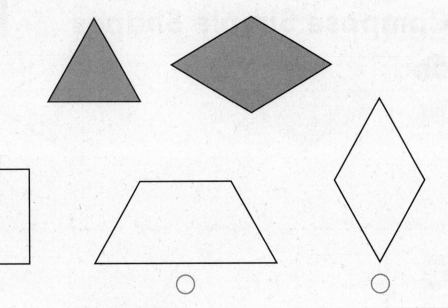

○   ○   ○

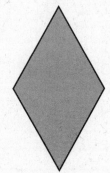 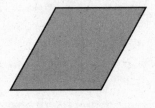 

Spiral Review

4. Mark under the shape that can be formed using the two gray shapes together.

5. Use the gray shapes shown to form the larger shape. Draw to show how you made the larger shape.

6. Circle the shape that is a cylinder.

Name _____

Compare Two-Dimensional and Three-Dimensional Shapes

    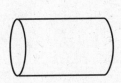

1. Mark an X on the three-dimensional shapes.
2. Color the two-dimensional shapes.
3. Color the three-dimensional shapes.
4. Circle the solid shape that has only flat surfaces.

Test Prep

 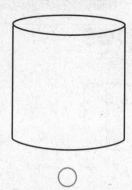 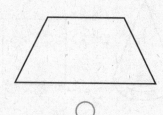 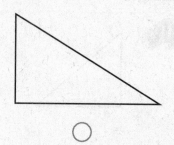

○　　　　　　○　　　　　　○

Spiral Review

5 Mark under the solid shape.
6 Circle the flat shape.
7 Circle the objects that are shaped like a sphere.

Compose Ten Ones and Some More Ones to 14

1 11   12   13   14

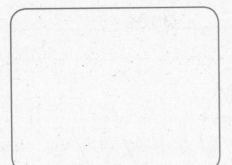

ten ones and _____ ones

2

14

_____ ones and _____ ones

---

1 Choose a number from 11 to 14 and circle it. The ten fish represent ten ones. Use those fish and draw some more ones to show the number you chose. Write the number to show how many more ones.

2 Circle ten objects. Then circle some more objects to represent the number. Write the numbers you used to represent the groups of objects.

Test Prep

 13 ○ ○ ○ ○ ○
○ ○ ○ ○ ○

ten ones and _____ ones

---

 12 △ △ △ △ △
△ △ △ △ △   △ △

○ 10 ones and 1 one

○ 10 ones and 2 ones

○ 10 ones and 4 ones

Spiral Review

 10, 20, 30, 40, _____, 60, 70, 80, 90, 100

© Houghton Mifflin Harcourt Publishing Company

---

3 The ten circles represent ten ones. Use those circles and draw more ones to show the number. Write the number to show how many more ones.

4 Mark to show the number of objects being represented.

5 Count by tens to 100. Write the number that comes after 40.

Name _____

Compose Ten Ones and Some More Ones to 15

1

15 ☐ ten ones and _____ ones

---

2   15

_____ ones and _____ ones

1 The ten baseballs at the top of the page represent ten ones. Use those baseballs and draw some more ones to show the number. Write the number to show how many more ones.

2 Circle ten objects. Then circle some more objects to show the number 15. Write the numbers you used to represent the groups of objects.

Module 17 • Lesson 2   one hundred sixty-seven **P167**

© Houghton Mifflin Harcourt Publishing Company

Test Prep

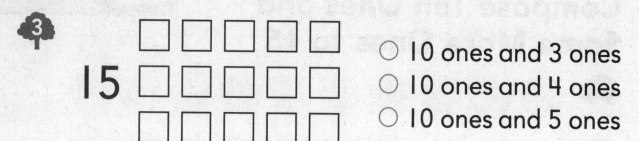

🌳 **3**

15

- ○ 10 ones and 3 ones
- ○ 10 ones and 4 ones
- ○ 10 ones and 5 ones

🐦 **4**

15

_____ ones and _____ ones

Spiral Review

⭐ **5**

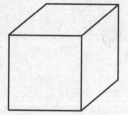 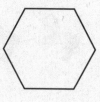 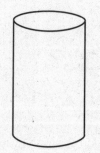

3 Mark to show the number of objects being represented.
4 Count the objects. Draw some more objects to show the number. Write the numbers you used to represent the groups of objects.
5 Color the three-dimensional shapes, or solids.

Compose Ten Ones and Some More Ones to 19

1.

19

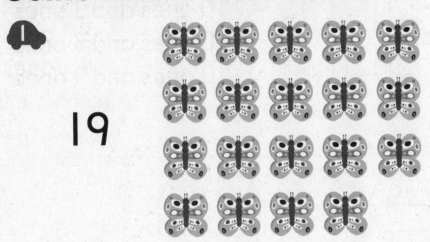

_____ ones and _____ ones

2.

| 16 | 17 | 18 | 19 |

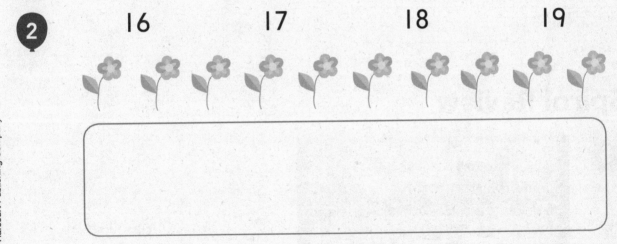

_____ ones and _____ ones

© Houghton Mifflin Harcourt Publishing Company

1. Circle ten objects. Then circle some more objects to represent the number. Write the numbers you used to represent the groups of objects.

2. Choose a number from 16 to 19 and circle it. The ten flowers represent ten ones. Use those flowers and draw some more ones to show the number you chose. Write the numbers to show ten ones and some more ones.

Test Prep

3

18

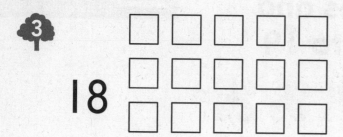

○ 10 ones and 3 ones
○ 10 ones and 8 ones
○ 10 ones and 9 ones

4

17

_____ ones and _____ ones

Spiral Review

5

---

3 Mark to show the number of objects being represented.

4 The ten shapes represent ten ones. Use those shapes and draw some more ones to show the number. Write the numbers to show ten ones and some more ones.

5 Mark an X on the object that is shaped like a sphere above the toy block.

Name _____

Represent Numbers to 20

1

20

2

17   15

---

3 18

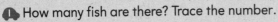

1. How many fish are there? Trace the number.
2. Count the frogs. Circle the number that shows how many.
3. Look at the number. Count as you draw to represent the number.

Test Prep

20

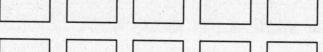

15   18   20
○   ○   ○

Spiral Review

     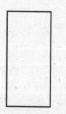

4 Count the circles. Count as you draw more circles to show 20. Trace the number.

5 Count the objects. Mark below the number that shows how many.

6 Mark an X on the cube that is next to the triangle.

LESSON 18.1
**More Practice/
Homework**

ONLINE
Video Tutorials and
Interactive Examples

Count and Write 11 to 14

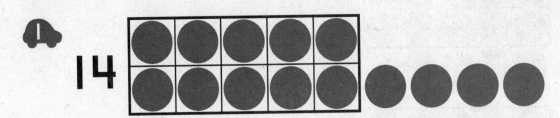

1. 14

$$14 = \underline{\hspace{1cm}} + \underline{\hspace{1cm}}$$

2.

3.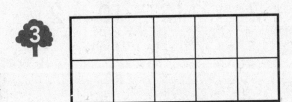

eleven _____

4.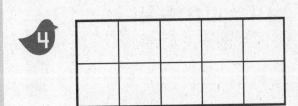

twelve _____

1. Count how many. Look at the ten counters and some more. Complete the equation.
2. Circle the group of stars that represents the number 13.
3. Draw counters to show eleven. Write the number.
4. Draw counters to show twelve. Write the number.

Test Prep

   •   • 12

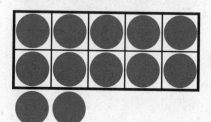   •   • 14

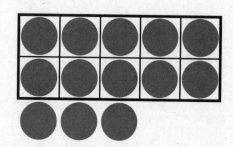

$$14 = 10 + 4 \qquad 13 = 10 + 3 \qquad 12 = 10 + 2$$

Spiral Review

ten ones and _____ ones

---

5. Draw lines to match each group of counters to the number they represent.

6. Mark below the equation that matches the counters.

7. Count the squares. Circle a group of ten squares. Write to show how many more ones.

LESSON 18.2
**More Practice/
Homework**

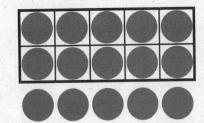

ONLINE
Video Tutorials and
Interactive Examples

Count and Write 15

 **1** 15

fifteen

$$10 + \underline{\hspace{2cm}} = \underline{\hspace{2cm}}$$

---

2 15

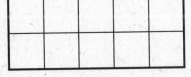   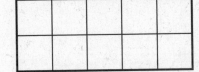

 3

---

1 Count how many. How can you represent the number? Complete the equation.
2 Circle the group of objects that represents the number.
3 How do you know you have 15 without counting every counter? Draw the counters in the ten frames to represent the number. Write the number.

Test Prep

15

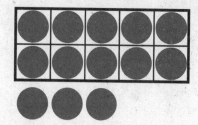 

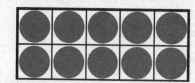   

$14 = 10 + 4$ $15 = 10 + 5$ $13 = 10 + 3$
○   ○   ○

Spiral Review

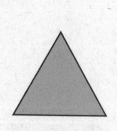   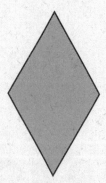   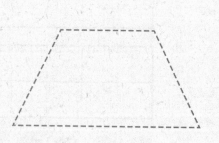

 Circle the picture that represents the number.

Mark below the equation that matches the counters.

Use the shapes shown to form the larger shape. Draw and color the shapes to show how you formed the larger shape.

Count and Write 16 to 19

 17
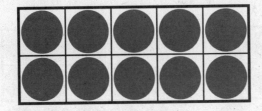

$$10 + \underline{\hspace{1.5cm}} = \underline{\hspace{1.5cm}}$$

2
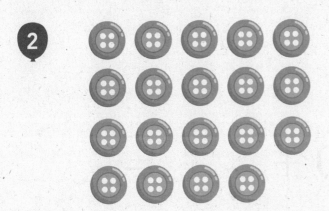
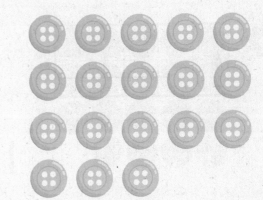

3
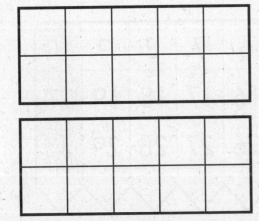

1. Count how many. Look at the ten counters and some more. Complete the equation.
2. Circle the group of objects that represents the number 19.
3. Suppose that children are planting flowers in rows of five or fewer. How would the garden look with 16 flowers? Draw in the ten frames to represent 16.

Test Prep

18

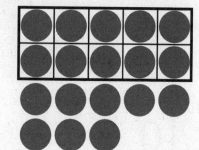

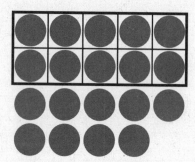

$$10 + \underline{\hspace{2cm}} = \underline{\hspace{2cm}}$$

Spiral Review

1	2	3	4	5	6	7	8	9	10
11	12	13	14	15	16	17	18	19	20
21	22	23	24	25	26	27	28	29	30

© Houghton Mifflin Harcourt Publishing Company

4. Say the number. Circle the group of objects that represents the number.
5. Complete the equation to match the counters.
6. Count by tens. Circle the number you count after 20.

Count and Write 20

 20

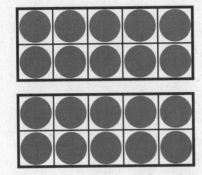
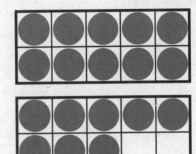

② **20**

③
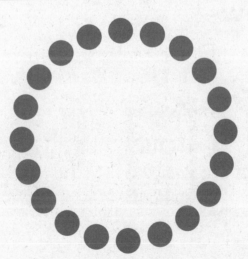

_____

❶ Say the number. Circle the group of objects that represents the number.
❷ Say the number. Draw to represent the number.
❸ Count how many. Write the number.

Test Prep

_____

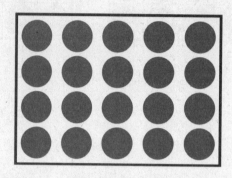

15   18   20

○   ○   ○

Spiral Review

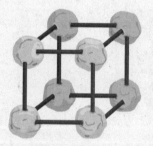         

---

4 Count how many. Write the number.

5 Mark below the number that represents how many counters.

6 Circle the real-world object that looks like the shape made from clay and sticks.

Describe Attributes of Length and Height

 1

 2

SHOE

1 Listen to the story. *Pedro has two pictures. He wants to put one picture in the frame.* How can you help Pedro find out which picture has about the same length and height as the picture frame? Circle the picture that will fit into the frame. Describe the lengths and heights of each picture.

2 Listen to the story. *Jordan wants to put one of the shoes in the box.* Use blue to show the length of each shoe. Use red to show the height of each shoe. Circle the shoe that could fit inside the box.

Test Prep

Spiral Review

15

_____ ones and _____ ones

---

3 Look at the pencil box. Circle the pencil that will fit in the box.

4 Look at the flower box. Circle the bunch of flowers that has about the same length and height as the box.

5 Circle ten objects. Then circle some more objects to show the number 15. Write the numbers you used to represent the objects.

Name _____

Compare and Describe Lengths

 1

2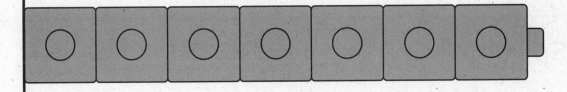

---

1. Look at the shovels. Use the words *longer than* or *shorter than* to compare the lengths of the shovels. Circle the longer shovel. Mark an X on the shorter shovel. Explain why the two shovels must be at the same starting point to compare the lengths.

2. Draw to show a cube train that is shorter than the one shown.

© Houghton Mifflin Harcourt Publishing Company

Test Prep

 3

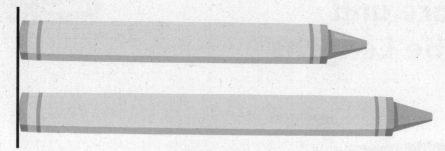

 4

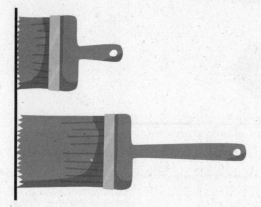

Spiral Review

 5

3 Listen to the story. Compare the lengths of the crayons. Circle to show which crayon Mia might use. *Mia likes to color with crayons. She likes to use long crayons. Which crayon might Mia use?*

4 Circle the longer paintbrush. Mark an X on the shorter paintbrush.

5 Count each group of flowers. Circle the group that has twenty flowers.

Name

Compare and Describe Heights

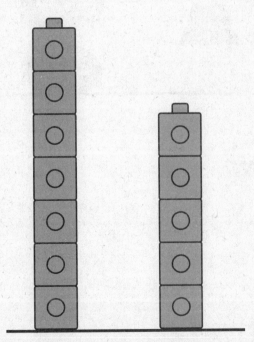

1. Look at the flowers. Use the words *taller than* or *shorter than* to describe the heights. Circle the taller flower. Mark an X on the shorter flower. Explain why the two flowers must be at the same starting point to compare the heights.

2. Listen to the story. Compare the heights of the cube towers. Circle to show which tower is shorter. *Ivan makes two cube towers. He wants to know which tower is shorter.*

Test Prep

Spiral Review

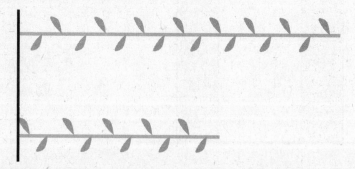

3 Compare the heights of the trees. Circle the taller tree. Mark an X on the shorter tree.
4 Compare the heights of the lamps. Circle the taller lamp. Mark an X on the shorter lamp.
5 Look at the vines. Compare the vines. Describe the vines using the words *longer than* or *shorter than* to describe the lengths. Circle the longer vine. Mark an X on the shorter vine.

Name _____

Describe Attributes of Weight

---

1. Look at the animals. Circle the animal that is heavy.
2. Look at the objects. Use the word *light* or *heavy* to describe the weight of each object. Mark an X on the object that is light.
3. Draw an object. Describe the weight of the object.

Test Prep

 4

 5

Spiral Review

 6

---

4 Describe the weight of the birds. Circle the bird that is heavy.

5 Describe the weight of the objects. Mark an X on the object that is light.

6 Draw to show a car that is shorter than the gray car.

Name _____

Compare and Describe Weights

 1

 2

 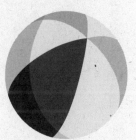

 3

---

1 Circle the object that has more weight, or is heavier.
2 Mark an X on the object that has less weight, or is lighter.
3 *Kelly bought two different-sized watermelons. She wants to serve the heavier one.*
Draw the two watermelons and circle the one Kelly serves.

Module 20 • Lesson 2   one hundred eighty-nine **P189**

Test Prep

Spiral Review

 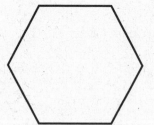 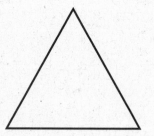

---

4 Circle the fruit that has more weight, or is heavier.
5 Mark an X on the object that has less weight, or is lighter.
6 Mark an X on the shape with six sides.

Name _____

Describe More Than One Attribute of an Object

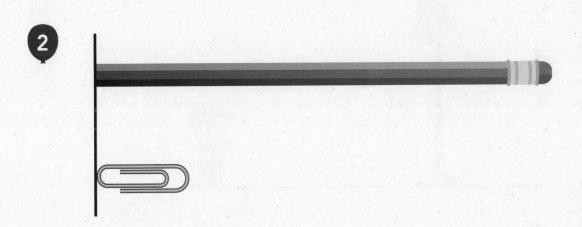

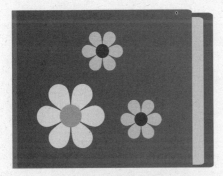

---

1. Draw an object that is short and light. Describe the height, length, and weight of the object.

2. Circle the object that is long and light.

3. *What are some different ways you can measure this book?* Use red to draw the line that shows how to measure length. Use blue to draw the line that shows how to measure height.

Test Prep

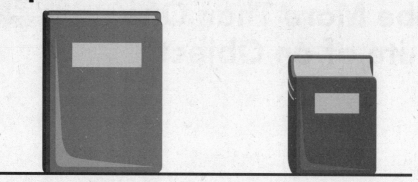

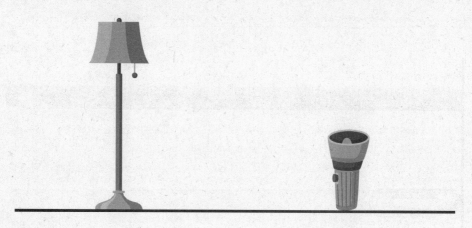

Spiral Review

4. Describe the height and weight of the books. Circle the book that is short and heavy.
5. Describe the height and weight of the objects. Circle the object that is tall and heavy.
6. Circle the animal that is heavy.

HMH | into Math™

My Journal

My Progress on Mathematics Standards
Correlations for *Into Math* Grade K

The lessons in your *Into Math* book provide instruction for Mathematics Standards for Grade K. You can use the following pages to reflect on your learning and record your progress through the standards.

As you learn new concepts, reflect on this learning. Consider inserting a check mark if you understand the concepts or inserting a question mark if you have questions or need help.

	Student Edition Lessons	My Progress
Domain: COUNTING AND CARDINALITY		
Cluster: Know number names and the count sequence.		
Count to 100 by ones and by tens.	9.1, 9.2	
Count forward beginning from a given number within the known sequence (instead of having to begin at 1).	9.3	
Write numbers from 0 to 20. Represent a number of objects with a written numeral 0–20 (with 0 representing a count of no objects).	2.1, 2.2, 2.3, 2.4, 8.1, 8.2, 8.3, 18.1, 18.2, 18.3, 18.4	

Mathematics Standards

	Student Edition Lessons	My Progress
Cluster: Count to tell the number of objects.		
Understand the relationship between numbers and quantities; connect counting to cardinality.		
• When counting objects, say the number names in the standard order, pairing each object with one and only one number name and each number name with one and only one object.	1.1, 1.2, 1.3, 1.4, 2.1, 2.2, 2.3, 2.4, 2.5, 7.1, 7.2, 7.3, 8.1, 8.2, 8.3, 8.4	
• Understand that the last number name said tells the number of objects counted. The number of objects is the same regardless of their arrangement or the order in which they were counted.	1.5, 2.1, 2.2, 2.3, 2.4, 8.1, 8.2, 8.3, 13.1, 13.2, 13.3, 13.4, 17.1, 17.2, 17.3, 17.4, 18.1, 18.2, 18.3, 18.4	
• Understand that each successive number name refers to a quantity that is one larger.	2.5, 3.1, 10.1	
Count to answer "how many?" questions about as many as 20 things arranged in a line, a rectangular array, or a circle, or as many as 10 things in a scattered configuration; given a number from 1–20, count out that many objects.	1.1, 1.2, 1.3, 1.4, 2.5, 7.1, 7.2, 7.3, 8.4, 17.1, 17.2, 17.3, 17.4, 18.4	

	Student Edition Lessons	My Progress
Cluster: Compare numbers.		
Identify whether the number of objects in one group is greater than, less than, or equal to the number of objects in another group, e.g., by using matching and counting strategies.	3.1, 3.2, 3.3, 3.4, 3.5, 10.1, 10.2, 10.3, 10.4, 10.5	
Compare two numbers between 1 and 10 presented as written numerals.	3.6, 10.6	
Domain: OPERATIONS AND ALGEBRAIC THINKING		
Cluster: Understand addition as putting together and adding to, and understand subtraction as taking apart and taking from.		
Represent addition and subtraction with objects, fingers, mental images, drawings, sounds (e.g., claps), acting out situations, verbal explanations, expressions, or equations.	5.1, 5.2, 5.5, 5.6, 6.1, 6.2, 6.5, 6.6, 11.1, 11.2, 11.3, 11.4, 11.5, 11.6, 11.7, 12.1, 12.2, 12.3, 12.4, 12.5	
Solve addition and subtraction word problems, and add and subtract within 10, e.g., by using objects or drawings to represent the problem.	5.1, 5.2, 5.3, 5.4, 5.5, 5.6, 5.7, 6.1, 6.2, 6.3, 6.4, 6.5, 6.6, 6.7, 11.1, 11.2, 11.3, 11.4, 11.5, 11.6, 11.7, 12.1, 12.2, 12.3, 12.4, 12.5	

	Student Edition Lessons	My Progress
Decompose numbers less than or equal to 10 into pairs in more than one way, e.g., by using objects or drawings, and record each decomposition by a drawing or equation (e.g., $5 = 2 + 3$ and $5 = 4 + 1$).	1.5, 13.1, 13.2, 13.3, 13.4	
For any number from 1 to 9, find the number that makes 10 when added to the given number, e.g., by using objects or drawings, and record the answer with a drawing or equation.	13.5	
Fluently add and subtract within 5.	5.7, 6.7	

	Student Edition Lessons	My Progress
Domain: NUMBER AND OPERATIONS IN BASE TEN		
Cluster: Work with numbers 11–19 to gain foundations for place value.		
Compose and decompose numbers from 11 to 19 into ten ones and some further ones, e.g., by using objects or drawings, and record each composition or decomposition by a drawing or equation (such as 18 = 10 + 8); understand that these numbers are composed of ten ones and one, two, three, four, five, six, seven, eight, or nine ones.	17.1, 17.2, 17.3, 17.4, 18.1, 18.2, 18.3	
Domain: MEASUREMENT AND DATA		
Cluster: Describe and compare measurable attributes.		
Describe measurable attributes of objects, such as length or weight. Describe several measurable attributes of a single object.	19.1, 20.1, 20.3	
Directly compare two objects with a measurable attribute in common, to see which object has "more of"/"less of" the attribute, and describe the difference. *For example, directly compare the heights of two children and describe one child as taller/shorter.*	19.2, 19.3, 20.2	

	Student Edition Lessons	My Progress
Cluster: Classify objects and count the number of objects in each category.		
Classify objects into given categories; count the number of objects in each category and sort the categories by count.	4.1, 4.2, 4.3, 4.4	
Domain: GEOMETRY		
Cluster: Identify and describe shapes.		
Describe objects in the environment using names of shapes, and describe the relative positions of these objects using terms such as *above*, *below*, *beside*, *in front of*, *behind*, and *next to*.	15.1, 15.2, 15.3	
Correctly name shapes regardless of their orientations or overall size.	14.1, 14.2, 14.3, 14.4, 16.1, 16.2, 16.3, 16.4, 16.5	
Identify shapes as two-dimensional (lying in a plane, "flat"), or three-dimensional ("solid").	14.1, 14.2, 14.3, 14.4, 16.7	

	Student Edition Lessons	My Progress
Cluster: Analyze, compare, create, and compose shapes.		
Analyze and compare two- and three-dimensional shapes, in different sizes and orientations, using informal language to describe their similarities, differences, parts (e.g., number of sides and vertices/"corners") and other attributes (e.g., having sides of equal length).	14.1, 14.2, 14.3, 14.4, 16.1, 16.2, 16.3, 16.4, 16.5, 16.7	
Model shapes in the world by building shapes from components (e.g., sticks and clay balls) and drawing shapes.	14.5, 16.1, 16.2, 16.3	
Compose simple shapes to form larger shapes. *For example, "Can you join these two triangles with full sides touching to make a rectangle?"*	16.6	

My Learning Summary

As you learn about new concepts, complete a learning summary for each module. A learning summary can include drawings, examples, non-examples, and terminology. It's your learning summary, so show or include information that will help you.

At the end of each module, you will have a summary you can reference to review content for a module test and help you make connections with related math concepts.

My Learning Summary

My Learning Summary

My Learning Summary

My Learning Summary

My Learning Summary

My Learning Summary

My Learning Summary

My Learning Summary

My Learning Summary

My Learning Summary

Name _____

My Learning Summary

Name _____

My Learning Summary

Name _____

My Learning Summary

My Learning Summary

My Learning Summary

My Learning Summary

My Learning Summary

My Learning Summary

My Learning Summary

Name

My Learning Summary

As you learn about each new term, add notes, drawings, or sentences in the space next to the definition. Doing so will help you remember what each term means.

A

	My Vocabulary Summary
above arriba, encima  The kite is **above** the rabbit.	
add sumar 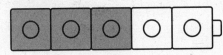 3 + 2 = 5	
addend el sumadol 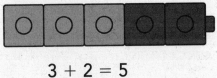 3 + 2 = 5 **addend**	

My Vocabulary Summary

Add To
ampliar

Two bunnies **add to** two bunnies for a total of four bunnies.

and
y

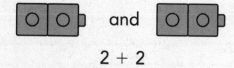

and

2 + 2

B

behind
detrás

The box is **behind** the girl.

My Vocabulary Summary

below

debajo

The rabbit is **below** the kite.

beside

junto a

The tree is **beside** the bush.

big

grande

big

C

My Vocabulary Summary

category
categoría

fruits

toys

circle
círculo

classify
clasificar

apples

not apples

My Vocabulary Summary

column
columna

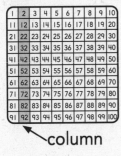

column

compare
comparar

cone
cono

corner
esquino

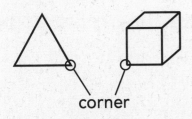

corner

My Vocabulary Summary

count
contar

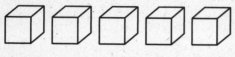

| 1 | 2 | 3 | 4 | 5 |

Count the number of cubes to find the total number.

cube
cubo

curved surface
superficie curva

Some solids have a **curved surface**.

cylinder
cilindro

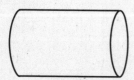

E

My Vocabulary Summary

eight

ocho

eighteen

dieciocho

eleven

once

equal to

igual a

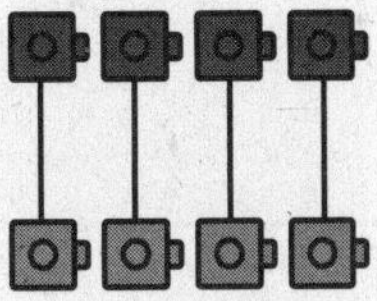

the number of cubes in
the top group is **equal to**
the number of cubes in the
bottom group

equation

la ecuació

$4 + 1 = 5$

F

My Vocabulary Summary

fifteen
quince

five
cinco

flat
plano

A circle is a **flat** shape.

flat surface
superficie plana

Some solids have a
flat surface.

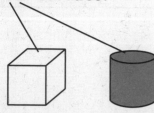

© Houghton Mifflin Harcourt Publishing Company

My Vocabulary Summary

four
cuatro

🔲🔲🔲🔲

fourteen
catorce

🔲🔲🔲🔲🔲🔲🔲🔲🔲🔲
🔲🔲🔲🔲

G

greater than
mayor que

🔲🔲🔲🔲🔲🔲 6
🔲🔲🔲🔲🔲🔲🔲🔲🔲 9

9 is **greater than** 6

H

heavier
más pesado

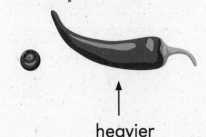

heavier

Interactive Glossary

My Vocabulary Summary

height

la altural

Height: the distance from top to bottom

---

hexagon

hexágono

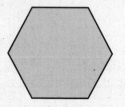

I

in front of

delante de

The box is **in front of** the girl.

My Vocabulary Summary

is equal to
es igual a

$$3 + 2 = 5$$

What is on the left side of the equal sign (=) **is equal to** what is on the right side of the equal sign (=).

J

join
juntar

$$2 + 1 = 3$$

L

larger
más grande

    2   **3**

A quantity of 3 is **larger** than a quantity of 2.

My Vocabulary Summary

length
el largo

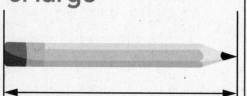

Length: the distance from one end of an object to the other

less than
mentos quel

 9

 11

9 is **less than** 11

lighter
más liviano

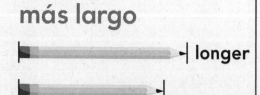

lighter

longer
más largo

longer

M

My Vocabulary Summary

match
emparejar

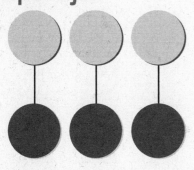

minus
menos

$$4 - 1 = 3$$

4 **minus** 1 is equal to 3

more
más

2 **more** leaves

N

My Vocabulary Summary

next to
al lado de

The bush is **next to** the tree.

nine
nueve

nineteen
diecinueve

O

one
uno

My Vocabulary Summary

ones
unidades

3 **ones**

P

plus
más

2 **plus** 1 is equal to 3
$2 + 1 = 3$

Put Together
armar

$2 + 2 = 4$

R

rectangle
rectángulo

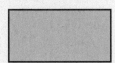

My Vocabulary Summary

row
fila

1	2	3	4	5	6	7	8	9	10
11	12	13	14	15	16	17	18	19	20
21	22	23	24	25	26	27	28	29	30
31	32	33	34	35	36	37	38	39	40
41	42	43	44	45	46	47	48	49	50
51	52	53	54	55	56	57	58	59	60
61	62	63	64	65	66	67	68	69	70
71	72	73	74	75	76	77	78	79	80
81	82	83	84	85	86	87	88	89	90
91	92	93	94	95	96	97	98	99	100

row →

S

seven
siete

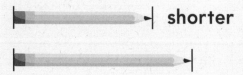

seventeen
diecisiete

shorter
más corto

shorter

My Vocabulary Summary

side
lado

side

six
seis

sixteen
dieciséis

size
tamaño

big   small

small
pequeño

small

My Vocabulary Summary

solid
sólido

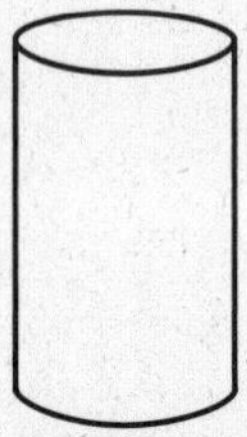

solid

A cylinder is a **solid** shape.

sort
ordenar

All of these
are gray.   All of these
are white.

You can **sort** these shapes.

sphere
esfera

square
cuadrado

My Vocabulary Summary

subtract
restar

3 − 1 = 2

T

Take Apart
desmontar

5 − 2 = 3

take away
para llevar

Take From
lievarse

3 − 1 = 2

© Houghton Mifflin Harcourt Publishing Company

My Vocabulary Summary

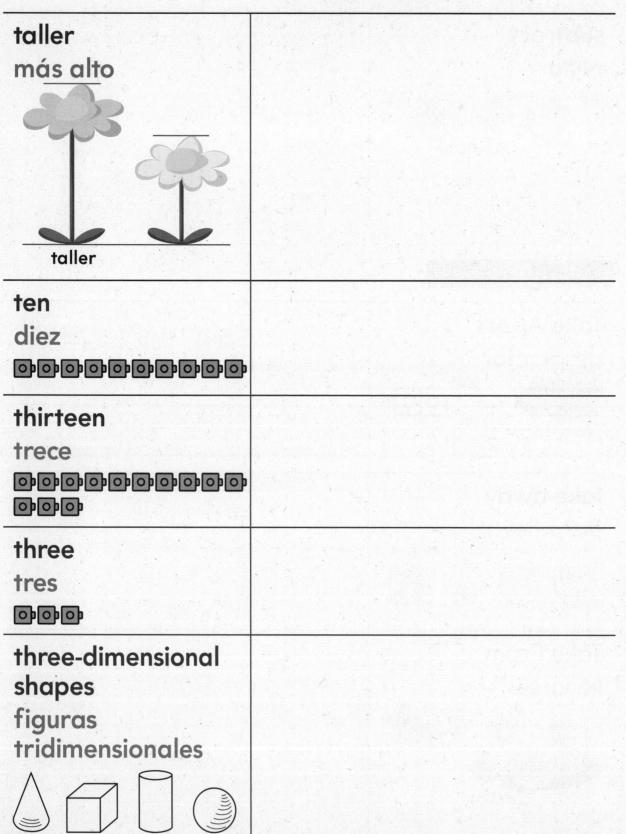

taller
más alto

taller

ten
diez

thirteen
trece

three
tres

three-dimensional shapes
figuras tridimensionales

My Vocabulary Summary

total

sumar

●● + ●●●● = ●●●●●●

2 + 4 = 6

total

Adding 2 marbles to
4 marbles makes a **total** of
6 marbles.

triangle

triángulo

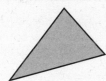

twelve

doce

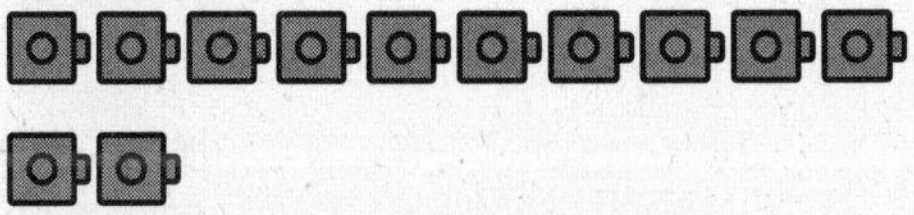

twenty

veinte

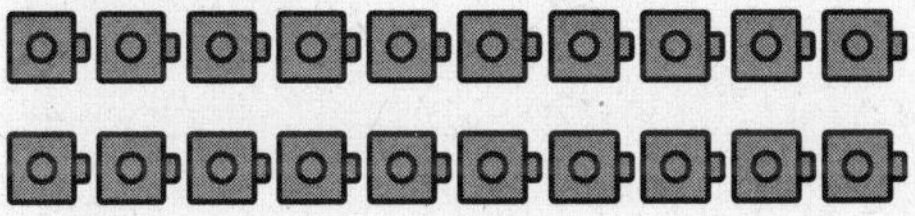

two

dos

My Vocabulary Summary

two-dimensional shapes
figuras bidimensionales

U

unknown
la incógnita

4 + ___ = 6

  + ___ =

V

vertex
vértice

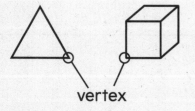

vertex